prairie silence

prairie silence

a memoir

Melanie M. Hoffert

Beacon Press, Boston

Beacon Press
25 Beacon Street
Boston, Massachusetts 02108-2892
www.bcacon.org

Beacon Press books
are published under the auspices of
the Unitarian Universalist Association of Congregations.

15 14 13 12   8 7 6 5 4 3 2 1

This book is printed on acid-free paper that meets the uncoated paper
ANSI/NISO specifications for permanence as revised in 1992.

Excerpts from the chapter "Silent Prairie Beginnings" were published as "Going
Home" in the Winter/Spring 2006 issue of the *Baltimore Review* and as "Prairie
Beginnings" in the 2009 issue of the *Mochila Review*; the chapter "The Allure of
Grain Trucks" was published in the 2009 issue of *Muse & Stone* and the 2010 issue
of *New Millennium Writings*. The community anthology *Wyndmere Centennial—June 28,
29, 30, 1985* (Gwinner, ND: J&M Printing, 1985) and *Wyndmere History in Review*
(privately published), the latter composed of articles by Dr. R. M. Johnson,
were the source for many facts about Wyndmere.

Text design by Kim Arney

Some names and identifying characteristics of people mentioned
in this work have been changed to protect their identities.

Library of Congress Cataloging-in-Publication Data

Hoffert, Melanie M.
Prairie silence : a memoir / Melanie M. Hoffert.
p. cm.
ISBN 978-0-8070-4473-5 (alk. paper)
1. Hoffert, Melanie M., 1974– 2. Lesbians—North
Dakota—Biography.
3. Coming out (Sexual orientation) I. Title.
HQ75.4.H64A3 2013
306.76'63092—dc23   2012010839

For my mom and dad
who probably got more than they bargained for—
and who love me all the same

Contents

The Allure of Grain Trucks   1

Silent Prairie Beginnings   21

Harvest Retreat   31

When Love Gains a Face   43

Rubbers and Nipples on the Farm   55

The Last Kiss   63

Yoga in the Air   73

Born Again for the First Time   83

Small-Town Tour   89

The Boy   99

Floating toward the Light   111

Redheaded Redneck   127

Bible Camp   137

God's Followers   155

The Plainness of Holiness   165

Grain Truck Apprenticeship   177

Sheets and Lights   189

Tiny Cowboy Town   199

Flow   211

The Last of the Barns   223

Epilogue: Going Home   233

Acknowledgments   237

The Allure of Grain Trucks

"Do you think it's weird that I want to drive a grain truck for a while?" my friend Melissa asks me over the phone.

"A grain truck? Seriously?" I tap my keyboard as I talk and notice that it is filthy, embarrassing almost. The keys are sticky and filled with crumbs. The entire board is splattered with coffee drips. *Disgusting*, I think.

I visualize Melissa, who is working in San Francisco, in a loft with high ceilings and little geometrical work stations lined with Macs. I imagine people wearing dark-rimmed eyeglasses, suit coats, torn jeans, and sneakers, popping their head into her office and flashing white smiles against tanned skin. Melissa herself is covered with tattoos and wears only eighties-vintage clothing, an appearance probably more reflective of her passion for music and pop culture than her day job at a publishing house.

In contrast my office is in a closed, dark corner of a building in St. Paul, just across the river from my home in Minneapolis. My walls are neutral. My plants are dying. My view is a parking lot. "Your very *own* office? Our baby girl is so important!" my mom would exclaim, not noticing the depressing vanilla walls, crusty plants, or uninspiring view—thrilled by the fact that her baby girl has somehow managed to find herself an executive position with all of the perks. And standing in my office she would grab a piece of paper and ask me about my job again, even though it has been several years since I've been here. "I *have* to get it right, honey. Everyone always asks me. I just tell them you do something with computers."

"Ma, I work *on* a computer. Everyone does." I've told her.

"Yes. Seriously," Melissa continues, breaking into my thoughts. "I was thinking I could come home—maybe just for a few months—and drive truck through harvest. I could live in that old farmhouse on my parents' land and then figure out what to do afterwards." She pauses. "You know—I think I'm just ready to get out. I'm ready to leave the city. Plus—seriously—how hard would it be to learn how to drive the truck again? I drove when I was fourteen!"

I am, I realize, slightly impressed that my modest friend used to drive a grain truck as a kid. As a child I drove tractors but never trucks. My dad propped me behind the wheel of his John Deere tractor when they were short of hired men. I pulled the coulter chisel, a giant rake-like appendage, to loosen the soil before plowing. But I never had to drive a truck, where you had to be tall enough to reach the clutch while managing the long stick shift.

"Oh, my God. You'd be fine." I give her the old 'you'd be fine' hand wave, as if she can see me. "Pick it back up in no time," I say.

Melissa and I are both children of the North Dakota prairie. She grew up in a tiny town, Northwood, population 959, near the northern border of the state. I grew up on a farm eight miles outside of Wyndmere, population 533, on the southern border at about the same longitude as Northwood. Both small towns have a railroad that runs through the center, a grain elevator, a gas station, a Catholic church on one side of town, a Lutheran church on the other, and a few bars in between. In fact, our hometowns fit the description of most North Dakota small towns.

"I can see you driving a grain truck." I continue, savoring the vision of my thirtysomething friend—a tattooed San Francisco DJ with dyed black hair—driving a grain truck down gravel roads. Then I imagine all of us—those who left North Dakota—coming back, settling in with the farmers, filling the small-town bars at night, Schmidt beer in hand, talking about literature and the grain markets.

"You can?" Melissa asks, in her typical soft and humble way, as if her ideas are never good until someone else agrees.

"Yes. In fact, maybe we should buy a little farm together. Drive truck for some cash." I grab a tissue and start working on a coffee blot on my keyboard while I consider our long-term options. "Yeah. Maybe you could start a band and play in the bars at night. I mean, what else is going on there? Um—*nothing.* You'd probably be a hit! Then, after harvest, we could take a road trip. Tour North Dakota. I'll be your crew." I pause, not quite sure if *crew* is the word I am looking for; I am not into the music scene and feel immediately not so hip. "Or—I'll do something. Carry your guitar? Play the drums? I don't know."

"Would you? Really? You'd come to North Dakota to be my *roadie?"* she laughs.

"Yes! I will. Why not?"

I think of my family farm during harvest right then, how harvest nights in the middle of the country seem almost cosmopolitan: bright, moving, awake, and alive. The moon glows like an orange pumpkin in the sky. Trucks light up the yard as they come in from the fields to empty their bounty. Once drained, they return to the dark night for another hit of golden crop from the combines. All of this activity stirs the crisp, corn-filled air, which makes it smell like someone is baking sweet corn muffins from somewhere deep within the earth. All the while, real cooking is happening inside, where Mom is making hamburgers and fried onions for my dad and brother, who will come in exhausted and dirty well past ten o'clock.

"You know, Mo, I think you should make the move." I turn my keyboard upside down and watch the crumbs fall out like dirty snow. "I think *we* should."

Melissa and I both left North Dakota after college and moved to the city where we hoped to find something that existed beyond the prairie. At the time, this *something* was unspeakable—our shared secret. But now that we are in our thirties, it just might be time to return home—at least for a sabbatical of some sort—and confront the reasons we left.

"Yes! I think it is time to change our lives!" Melissa cheers in her calm way.

"I know. I could really use a break from work. From life. From the traffic and the busyness. I mean, how long can we go on like this?" I am being dramatic now, resorting to our college chatter. It is easy to fall into this lingo with Melissa. In college we spent long nights together in her small, carpeted apartment, talking about our lives. She played her electric guitar without an amp. I sat across from her on her ragged couch, chewing sunflower seeds and spitting them into a blue mug. The next morning we would do the same. She sat in her ripped pajamas, picking at her electric guitar, and I drank coffee from the same blue mug. I often crashed for the night at her place, too tired to drive across town to my own bed in a small house I shared with three other women. I am about to remind her of this, of our time together, when someone pops a frenzied head in my office.

"Hey, ah, you got a minute?"

I keep my eyes on the intruder and switch to my I-am-at-work-and-trying-to-be-professional voice, which I can barely pull out for Melissa. "Excuse me, Melissa. Can I interrupt you for just one minute? Yes. Sorry. I have a colleague at my door and have to run. Let's talk soon and *seriously* consider our"—I look at the person standing in my door—"our future business proposition."

She gets my drift. "Oh, sure. Yes. Call me later."

After I deal with the person who wants to know if I can set up a meeting to discuss something we had just discussed, I look out of my window. I notice the landscape: the parking lot, the cement, the buildings, the way my eye is stopped by a delivery truck, blocking my view of the earth.

I am lucky, aren't I? Let's add it up. One: in my thirties and successful for my age, with a team of thirty and budget of millions.

Two: a life in the city, with a home, a great relationship, and immediate access to restaurants and film. Three ... three—what is *three?*

I am happy, right? Why then does the thought of listening to AM radio and pulling my truck up to a grain elevator in a small North Dakota town have my heart fluttering with excitement? Why does the vision of sitting in a little North Dakota bar hitting a tambourine against my thigh, while Melissa sings to a crowd of men in John Deere hats and women in oversized sweatshirts, make me ache with purpose?

I throw my tissue away, take a breath, accept my dirty keyboard, and go back to work. Both Melissa and I know that our daydream of another life—in this case, returning to a past life—will probably only carry us through the next hour. Returning home is impossible.

Over the last ten years I have been trying to resolve a seemingly simple dilemma: how to tell the state of North Dakota that I am gay. This might sound crazy, but if you are from the heart of the country you might understand that you are part of a world that is more connected than any social networking phenomenon of the digital age. Your personal profile is peeked at, commented on, and updated at every hometown shower, funeral, wedding, pig roast, street dance, and Sunday-morning church service—even if you don't live in the small town anymore.

Living in the city I've learned that it is possible to retreat from the world and become anonymous. The more people, the more control I have over my identity—even to the point of erasing it. Yet I can never escape the world where I am from. Every Sunday morning Jerome, the plump man at church, asks my mom how I'm doing. My high school teacher still remembers the state speech award I received in eleventh grade. My neighbor Arlene sends me cards inviting me to stop by for homemade buns the next time I am home. I no longer live with these people, but they still live with me. I will never be anonymous, and yet—I will never be known either.

In this part of the world, if you have a secret, it does not necessarily belong to you or your family or even God. It belongs to the place you are from, because eventually to resolve everything, to truly find peace, you must come to terms with the place your inner soul calls home. In my case, this place is the North Dakota prairie.

The longer I drag my feet on this issue—my confession—the fewer people there are left to tell. Rural North Dakota—well, the whole middle of the country for that matter—has been emptying faster than the draining of a butchered cow. A 2008 *National Geographic* issue ran an article called "The Emptied Prairie," which featured the rural areas of my home state in a painfully irreversible population decline. The pictures in the article showed abandoned farmhouses in hauntingly dilapidated conditions, barren except for a few signs of life: a dusty doll, a white nightgown hanging in a bare room, an old woman looking forlorn out of a window onto the empty prairie. The pictures reminded me of villages left behind after military raids: one minute there is life and normalcy, the next minute there is stillness and emptiness.

Some attribute this loss to economics or lack of opportunity for young people. I think this emptying—at a cellular or even metaphysical level—has something to do with an even deeper issue: prairie silence.

To the good North Dakotans, my current life resembles something they might describe as a spinster's life. I am past thirty, independent, the oldest in my family, not married (of course), and I live with two cats. I refuse to get three for fear that I might graduate from spinster lady to cat lady, a far worse label.

"You met a fella yet?" The North Dakotans started asking every time I returned home to visit my family. I think they assumed

I had ventured into the world to find what used to be down the gravel road, working in the neighbor's barn: a good man.

"Ah. No. Nope. No." I'd respond in a nervous babble, trying to act normal even while my breathing changed to panic-attack shallow and I started screaming at the innocent questioner in my mind. *Good Lord, do not go there. Please. Please talk about your crops or the latest funeral or the church turkey supper. Anything else but the fella!* There was simply no way for me to tell them the truth.

And because they assumed comforting words were in order, they offered the following: "Well. This day and age? People are getting married later and later. Pretty gal like you? You'll find someone. A good one. You won't be alone for long!"

I have never been as alone as it may appear to the North Dakotans. When I first moved to the city, meeting people was like watching Mom unpack ornaments for our Christmas tree. She would sink her hands deep into the plastic tub and slowly pull small figures out of crinkly tissue paper, retrieving wiry stars, handmade decorated gingerbread cookies sprayed and preserved, colorful little quilted balls, and baby Jesuses with chipped cheeks. Each ornament had its own color, texture, history, and story. Similarly, in the city I met people making art, people with exotic pasts; I witnessed lives being pulled together, lives being torn apart. I experienced, for the first time, a taste of the world beyond farm life.

I also had a very active nightlife, exploring the world of *the gays*, as it might be called on the prairie. On Saturday nights beautiful and mysterious women sauntered into bars. I watched the parade, completely captivated: there were the hipsters, the academics, the granolas, and the tomboys. They were all shapes, sizes, and colors, with one common trait: confidence. *Where do they all come from*, I wondered. *Not from North Dakota*, I thought.

Before moving to Minneapolis I had experienced only the Fargo Bowler, where once a month they held underground, gay "Deca Dances." On those nights I watched the crowds of flannel-clad older women, skinny gay men, and college ravers (who were not gay but claimed the space as an alternative stomping ground) to find someone a bit younger, a bit more like me. I had a vision, I think, of someone who looked like my childhood best friend: someone with an athletic body, feminine disposition, a strong will, bright eyes, and dark hair. I, myself, would have probably fit in better at the sorority parties, with my lipstick, my eyeliner. I had been groomed to be this way—feminine, colorful, a perfect contrast for my prom dates in their black-and-white tuxes. I watched the women at these Deca Dances drink beer and scan the crowds. Ironically, the scene reminded me of a table filled with men at a small-town cafe. I did not yet understand the subtleties of gender politics or butch-femme dynamics or how later similar women would take me under their wing. At the time I simply wasn't interested in dating older women who still reminded me of a *fella*.

Today I prefer evenings with a bath and a book to those out on the town. I have settled into a relationship with Nancy, a woman I consider my partner though we don't live together. On evenings when we are together we talk about life, linger in our yards, or pick at our gardens. Often we make slow meals with fresh herbs, sizzling garlic, and sweet onions, mixing ingredients until the house fills with delicious and complex aromas. On these nights I am not alone. I am not a spinster. Yet this would be news back home.

A few years ago, when my sister announced her wedding engagement, I requested that she substitute my maid of honor title with a new title of my own creation: best sister. I knew at her wedding I would be encountering everyone from my past—those who had known me since I was in diapers but who had never once asked me if I am gay. The "best sister" title was a tiny act of public rebellion on my part, as if to tell North Dakotans that I will not be understood or defined by my marital status.

As we lined up to enter the church on her wedding day, sweat poured down my chest. I wasn't worried about my shoes, my dress, crying, or how my sister looked—which I think was supposed to be part of my job. I also wasn't worried about tripping, an issue that likely posed a real threat. Instead I was worried only about the programs, those two hundred little pieces of paper floating in the audience, now converted to fans and rolled up into little tubes, stuffed into pockets and shoved into hymnals. *They know! They know! They finally know!* Then I asked myself, sarcastically, *What actually do they know?* A response came from nowhere. *That I'm different!* And right then I felt liberated. My step became confident. I held my flowers tightly, and proudly marched toward the altar as if I was finally going to marry my truth.

As my sister and her soon-to-be husband exchanged vows, I decided to tune out the whole thing about woman being derived from man's rib, which always made me visualize human ribs coated in barbecue sauce. Instead I practiced how I would respond when my old neighbors and teachers and pastors and high school friends made wisecracks about my "best sister" title. "Yes, I decided to become a best sister because I will not be defined by my relationship status," I'd tell them. And while they would stand there—confused—because what I've said doesn't make a lick of sense, I would tap my chin, as if just hit with the most random thought: "Say, along those lines, for about twenty years—well, my whole life really—I have been meaning to tell you that I prefer to date women."

Good North Dakotans, if you must know, would usually make a smart comment. "Best sister, eh? What, 'cha get a medal or something? Win some sort of award in the big city?" Then they'd grab me around the shoulder, clunk my drink with their plastic beer cup, squeeze me, and say "Cheers!" as if to say, *Just teasing, kiddo.* They'd make a comment—that is, unless they didn't want to hear a response.

That night when the band started to play and the dance unfolded as most small town wedding dances do, I waited and watched. Old people sat around the perimeter of the dance floor on folding chairs, drinking coffee and visiting. Little kids chased each other, screaming like baby hyenas. Women kicked off their shoes. Men loosened their ties. People pulled me out to dance and bounced me around like a tetherball. The night unfolded as planned, but nobody brought up "best sister." Realizing that nobody was going to confront me, I took big gulps of my gin and tonic and relaxed. My shoulders fell, my chest became light. I slid across the dance floor and looped arms with family and people I've known since childhood. I welcomed, once again, the familiar and numbing comfort of our silence.

Melissa and I became friends in college during one of the worst winters in North Dakota history. It was in 1997, the year when melting snowdrifts—some crashing like waves over houses and cars—created record spring flooding in the Red River Valley. Fargo officials ordered residents to stay inside, out of the 80-degree-below windchill. Anyone who disobeyed, they threatened on TV, would receive a ticket.

Knowing we would be locked in our house for days when the blizzards hit, my three roommates and I scurried to the grocery store in our parkas and our flannel pajamas to stock up on food and other supplies. Melissa, at first a friend of one of my roommates, drove from her tiny apartment on the other side of town, not wanting to be alone during the storm. While big flakes fell from the sky, we took naps, cooked frozen pizzas, made pancakes, and flipped to the weather station to get updates between movies. The little house was barely big enough for one person, let alone five. But this was college, when a house filled with friends was more important than a house filled with space and nice furniture. We ignored time over those long days, which I now realize is a rare gift of a contented mind.

Melissa, a quiet girl who wanted to be a musician, worked at the Fargo Theatre, where you could catch independent films. She wore jeans, button-up shirts over band T-shirts, and pulled her hair up on each side of her head, clipping it with a single barrette. She also wore Dr. Martens, which struck me as a tiny statement of artistic rebellion because at the time they were the boots of the theater majors, not North Dakota farm girls.

On one of the blizzard nights, when my roommates went to bed early, Melissa changed the course of our relationship. The house was quiet. Melissa and I were playing cards under the glow of red Christmas lights. She tossed me the question as freely as she tossed me a king of spades. "Are you a heartbreaker?"

As soon as the words left her lips my palms began to sweat. At that time not even my roommates knew I was gay.

"That's a strange question. What do you *mean*?" I said, grabbing her king, pretending to be consumed with our game.

"Why is it strange? Because you are one?" Her voice was serious.

"Are one—what?"

"A heartbreaker! Are you a heartbreaker?" I sat up straight in my chair. The quiet girl who barely said a word when she was at our house asked this with such intensity and directness that it was as if another person had just entered the room and stepped into her body. I wasn't sure where to go with her question. Beside it being rather odd, it was also as if she was accusing me of something.

"I . . . wouldn't . . . say . . . so, exactly," I responded cautiously. She just stared at me. "I mean, no. No! I am not a heartbreaker. Why are you asking?"

"Really? What would *Samantha* say?" A cold wind seemed to shake the house. Samantha was the first woman I had dated at college. My relationship with her had been the antithesis of what I had imagined a relationship with a woman would be. It had ended two years earlier. I certainly hadn't broken her heart. In fact, I thought she had crushed mine.

Where might this be going? I wondered. I could understand Melissa fishing for a confession of my secret life, one that I had

shared with only a handful of new friends. But Melissa's accusa-
tions seemed to be less about me being gay than me being a
heartbreaker. I didn't understand.

"Frankly, I don't care what Samantha says," I responded, and
put down another card. "So, you obviously must know her?"

"Yes. She knows my roommate Laura."

"Oh. So you must know a lot about me then," I said, my heart
pounding now. I was unpracticed, still frozen when it came to talking about my desire to be in a relationship with a woman. I tried
to act calm, as if I had been through this discussion a hundred
times. "Did Samantha say I am a heartbreaker or something?"

Melissa didn't respond. Instead she got up and went to the
couch, sat, pulled her knees close to her chest, and rocked back and
forth. Her face turned white. I followed her. I was confused, scared,
and curious. I was the one who was now exposed. I was the one
with the secret! Why was she shaking like a small hurt animal?

"Are you okay?" I asked. Then they came: words flowed
from her like lava that had been waiting a thousand years to
touch the air. She was shaking, spilling stories of a longtime love
affair with her female basketball coach from high school. The
woman, now a coach at a nearby college, had ended their
several-year-long relationship.

Melissa's interrogation was not about me—it was about her.
Her accusation of me quickly fizzled as her more authentic need
emerged: the need to share her story before she bled to death in-
ternally. Like me, she kept her feelings a secret, one she did not
share with another living soul, not her family, not her friends, not
her small town. Her fear forced her to deal with the most dramatic
and painful experience of her young life—the loss of a first love—
in complete silence. I had done the same, years earlier. Melissa
had decided that the demise of her pure love could only be explained by thinking of her ex-love as someone she didn't really
know, someone capable of being a heartbreaker.

On that blizzard night we talked until dawn, putting words to
years of silence, like finally putting words to a musical score. And

over the next year, our senior year, Melissa became my closest friend. She ventured with me to the Fargo Bowler, where we danced into the night with women and men who came from nowhere and disappeared into that nowhere when the night ended.

Melissa and I both left the prairie after college, convinced we were the only lesbians in North Dakota younger than fifty. Melissa moved to San Francisco, learned how to DJ, started a band, and joined the hipster counterculture queers in the Mission. I moved to Minneapolis, focused on my career, bought a house, and started graduate school. Melissa and I took different paths but are still connected by our beginning, a beginning we both still crave.

Shortly after she moved, Melissa got the outline of North Dakota—with a tiny star marking the location of Northwood—tattooed on her wrist. Next she got the word *Heartland* down the middle of her arm. In ways the tattoos symbolize how far she's grown from her farming roots, as well as how deeply rooted she really is.

Some living in the state are trying to put a tourniquet on the gaping wound through which many educated and ambitious young people leave. And even though the *National Geographic* article generated letters from angry North Dakotans wanting to defend the viability and fruitfulness of the state, and despite the fact that since 2008 an oil boom in the Bakken Formation has attracted an influx of people to the Minot area, I doubt the most optimistic North Dakotan could ever imagine a restoration of rural America, of towns with populations ranging from thirty to two thousand. The small town, it seems, is dying into extinction.

Of my family, one out of four of us stayed on the farm in North Dakota. I am the oldest; David follows; my sister, Chrisy, is also tucked in the middle; and Donny is the baby. We didn't know, early on, which one of us might stay on the land. I might have thought David, since he is the oldest boy and has my father's disposition: quiet, clever, determined, and stubborn. If given a few tools and raw materials, he can create or fix just about anything.

But David ended up going to school, getting married, and moving to Fergus Falls, Minnesota—a midsize town—where he manages the e-commerce website for a retail store. My sister would never have stayed to work on the farm—as girls we were not expected to be farmers—but she might have stayed in the area, close to family and friends. Her goal was always to become a mom, and she did, but not in North Dakota. She moved to Washington State. Both David and Chrisy, like me, have lives away from the farm. Donny is the only one of us who stayed close to the earth. He became a farmer.

There are 68,994 square miles in North Dakota and 642,200 people—about nine people per square mile. In Minneapolis, there are about 1,800 people per square mile. Sometimes at dusk, when the world is purple, I go searching for elements of a small town in the city. I usually walk down alleys, where yellow light spills from the back of houses onto piles of dusty red bricks and onto old lumber, where forgotten white Christmas lights crawl like vines over many of the fences, where junk cars sit as if in a museum, and where recycling bins display evidence of meals consumed weeks ago. In alleys people do not have a need to present a manicured life, and I feel closer to the neighbors I will never know. In these alleys, where the roads are narrow and life is presented as it is lived—messy and whimsical—I see glimpses of what I left behind.

I have learned that the one personal revelation that will cause pause—when I am on a business trip to New York, for example—is not about dating women. The eyebrow-raiser is this: "I'm originally from North Dakota."

"North Dakota?" My new acquaintances always repeat my statement in the form of a question, as if I must have been mistaken.

"North Dakota," I will say with a shrug.

"Wow!" They tilt their heads. "*Really?*"

"Yes. Really."

At this point they'll get a smug grin. "Now tell me. What in the world is North Dakota like?" As if I am about to deliver the punch line.

This is a difficult question for me to answer. Somehow I want to explain to them that the land is beautiful, beyond their imagination. But I am stopped, like when I bring my city friends back to the farm. When the houses thin and we are eventually surrounded by nothingness I suddenly lose my vision. The world looks bleak, flat, unpromising, and colorless. I start apologizing as if I had dragged them to an empty art gallery. "The view is kind of ugly this time of year," I'll say.

I am often taken aback at my own hesitancy to claim roots in North Dakota. When asked where I'm from I feel unavoidably self-conscious, wanting to immediately say, "Well, I've moved," or to make other disclosures to separate me from my past. Though they don't say it, when people look at me with their curious smirks I assume they envision a desolate land, a place without beauty, culture, or even purpose. I've backpacked through Colorado, gone from rim to rim in the Grand Canyon, sat on glaciers in Alaska, nestled in lodges at Yellowstone, and spent time on both coasts. I have observed how people flock to quaint tourist towns like Jackson, Wyoming, or Park City, Utah. I understand the compulsion well, wanting to get away from clutter and noise, crime and pollution. Yet these spaces are inhabited by people who can afford to buy space and beauty, many of whom have no need to understand the earth in order to survive.

Yet when I return to the farm on my own and am not responsible for another person's experience, the land speaks to me in another way. Rediscovering the landscape of North Dakota is like finding a familiar childhood book with soft pages that smell sweet with age. The flat land is not dry, not dark, not lifeless. Instead, North Dakota is a painter's palette where all of the earthly colors settle. The light changes minute by minute, following unassuming subjects: a wheat field, a gravel road, a gray grain elevator. When I squint I can almost see the bottom of glacial Lake Agassiz, the ancient lake that left the Red River Valley fertile and flat. The rows in the fields are the sand ripples of the lake bottom. The shelterbelts are large, alien sea plants, reaching to the light. The sky is the surface of the lake reflecting the sun.

"North Dakota is actually very beautiful," is all I will say to my new acquaintances. They'll look at me with a suspicious eye as if to say, "What could emptiness possibly hold?"

They are right about emptiness, at least.

Over the years, I came home to find that not only had businesses closed, they were actually gone. Completely vanished. Today my hometown's main street resembles the mouth of an old woman who is missing most of her teeth. A few brick buildings still stand, surrounded by spaces that will never be filled.

I cannot say why, exactly, it matters that these buildings are gone, though I think it has something to do with driving through any part of the country and being solicited by the same chain stores with the same brands with the same colors and the same goods, whether you are in Arizona or Minnesota. The only difference in some of these places is the natural world, the lakes and the cacti, reminding us of contrast, of hot and cold, of mountains and valleys. I frequent the assimilated superstores—they have trained me to know their aisles, to be thankful that in a hurried stop I can retrieve Glad trash bags or Tide by walking straight for four aisles and turning left, whether I am in Utah or Ohio.

Or maybe it matters that these businesses are gone because of the people, something to do with visions of my parents' friends, business owners and farmers, who took jobs in larger towns pushing paper and drinking coffee out of Styrofoam cups, making small talk with coworkers and answering to a boss in a stale, fluorescent-lit office.

As I ponder those of us who have left the prairie, I wonder what stories we take with us and what longer stories we end. There are, of course, those few kids who don't end up leaving the prairie. They are the ones who take over family businesses or marry their high school sweethearts. These people become the material of the next generation, the thin fabric that keeps the community connected and viable. Of those who do leave, I think there are two manifestations. First, there are the few who leave early and permanently. They escape into the larger world and truly disappear. Their faces are forever frozen in high school yearbooks. Then, there are the rest of us. The in-betweens. We leave, but we never truly leave. Our families are rooted in the community like the trees are rooted in the earth. We are connected to this place we still call home, to people we call neighbors and friends. But some of us must keep the familiar at arm's length because of prairie silence.

Prairie silence is—I have come to believe—the way the people of the prairie mirror the land with their sturdy, hardworking, fruitful, and quiet dispositions. They are committed to each other like the soil is committed to the crop. They are uncomplaining, in the way the land dutifully recovers after tornadoes, droughts, and floods destroy a season's harvest. They are humble and quiet, like white prairie grass in the wind. They swallow their problems, their fears, their shames, and their secrets—figuring that nature will take care of everything, somehow or other. That is, after all, how it works with the crops. And once a silence has taken hold, whatever it is, it is hard to uproot.

I haven't always been fond of the farm. As a child I made a stink about living in the middle of nowhere. I made sure Mom knew how unfair it was that the town kids had to ride their bikes only a few blocks to see friends. I had to ride mine at least three miles.

"Honey, believe me, you wouldn't like to live in town—all those people," my mom would say. She was the authority, the only one in my family who had ever lived in a town, having grown up in Wahpeton, North Dakota. "Plus, you can play with the Holtzes anytime you like."

The Holtz kids lived three miles down the gravel road, a good bike ride away, and could have very well lived in the trees. They were stocky and strong, three boys and a girl, with deep, gravelly laughs, freckles, dark hair, and eyes lit with a sort of devious, wild joy. At their farm my brother and I spent hours riding in creaky wagons connected to lawn-mower engines the Holtzes had turned into small vehicles. The Holtzes were like pirates on the sea, piled up on their small tractor, with headbands and beautifully tanned faces, looking into the horizon, and pulling us down well-worn paths they had carved into the shelterbelts by their farm.

The Holtz kids were earth kids. They belonged in the trees. In another time and place they would have settled on the land—I am quite sure—connected by a deep and long tradition, by a pulse running through their blood. Yet their parents moved before the oldest of the Holtzes was old enough to go to high school. My brother and I were devastated to lose the only friends we could visit without having to get into a car. Today all of the Holtz kids live in towns far away from their small farm—far from the abandoned paths they carved into the trees such a long time ago.

Sometimes I wonder if I will be the last generation of my family to live on the land, to know the land. And sometimes I wonder if I am the first generation of a larger kind: the first generation of people to finally and permanently leave the land, the small towns, and the Lutheran churches where they still make coffee by mixing a raw egg with the grounds. The first generation to realize that the world of rural America—both the good and the bad of it—will never again be as it once was. The first generation to look back and say, with sadness, *I cannot return.*

Is silence, *my* silence, this powerful? Maybe.

Even so, on the day I talked on the phone with Melissa about a "business proposition," the idea of returning to the farm entered my thoughts like a rock I'd found on the beach and slipped into my pocket. From that day forward, despite having the life I was supposed to want—living comfortably, with a good job, surrounded by progressive thinkers, traveling to New York for work—I began to catch myself daydreaming about adjusting the dial of the AM radio in a bouncing truck, drinking Schmidt beer while farmers boast of their crops, and exploring the remnants of crumbling towns. Little did I know that a plan was brewing inside of me—and that in a couple of years I would return home for a harvest and be changed forever.

Silent Prairie Beginnings

My relationship with prairie silence began at age four near our little green house on my great-uncle's farmstead. On the farm there were several wooden sheds, my great-aunt's strawberry garden, their house, and ours. During those years I spent my days sitting on our wooden front step and exploring the trees next to our house. In the late summer, butterflies filled the air, floating above tall prairie weeds. My dad, uncle, grandpa, and great-uncle worked like couriers as they moved machinery from our yard to my grandpa's farm, just a mile down the road, where my parents would build our new house a couple of years later.

Growing up I believed this was all there was to life: the farm, the wind, the silence. Yet while I was sitting on our front step, feeding my cats and watching farm machinery move from the farmyard, the rest of the world was pulsing. Cities were crawling with people. The world was buzzing with the aftermath of Watergate and Nixon's impeachment. The Vietnam War had recently come to an end. I was in my twenties before I decided to figure out what *Watergate* even meant.

I also did not understand then that the landscape of my early years, a place where people still follow instinct—relying on the smell of the early morning or the behavior of animals to predict rain or tornadoes—will call to me for the rest of my life.

When I go back to visit the farm I often walk to the old graveyard at the Homestead Church, which is only a few yards from our present-day farmhouse, a seventies, split-level home, and a mile from the little green house that was bulldozed long ago. The wind will seem to come from nowhere at the graveyard, changing directions almost viciously, thrusting me—and the trees—in the direction of its force. When I close my eyes I listen to the wind dancing with the pine trees, bartering for control. The trees and the wind go through this ritual, pushing, pulling, honoring each other's strength, each refusing to surrender. Here, I believe—with eyes closed, my body conceding to the wind—is where I first heard the ocean. Like the coil of a shell's spiral carries the echo of the ocean, so too does the prairie wind mimic the sea as it begs its way through the needles of the graveyard pines.

Since childhood I have visited the graves of prairie people I know only by the shapes of their headstones, the year spans of their lives, and the small inscriptions that mark their time on earth: Beloved, Mother, Father, Wife, Husband. Before we settled in our little house, there were others here: generations of families that came to the prairie to make a life. And though life has often seemed forever expansive, particularly when I was a child visiting these graves, the headstones have stayed with me as a haunting reminder that in the end, all of our longings, fears, loves, and silences may be summarized by a few words chosen by other people and etched into stone.

At the graveyard I often picture the early women of North Dakota, robust and strong, with thick, pear-shaped bodies, wide hips, powerful arms, and solid legs. Their bodies, as if selected in an evolutionary twist particular to the north, were built to endure cold winters, long harvests, and the repeated cycle of childbirth. They were proud of their strength and honored for it. Their families depended upon their ability to plow a field when their husbands fell ill. Like the unjustly displaced Native American women who lived on the plains before them, they understood the temperaments and intricacies of the land. They had to know the land to survive.

The women I knew as a child, the white-haired women of the small Lutheran church, wearers of sensible SAS shoes, were variations on this archetype. They were short, stocky, and their skin was weathered in a way that seemed to suggest it had with-stood years of harvest sun and heat, relentless winds, and sub-zero temperatures. The oldest of the old retained their Norwegian or German accents, a clue to me that they were connected to another land.

I think of these women—those I knew and those I imag-ined—when I study my body. Some women seem to dance as they walk; their slender legs and long arms make them more like crea-tures of the sky, as if they might flutter away if the hand of Peter Pan appeared. My body, however, has often seemed to me to be bound to the earth: low, centered, and solid. When I look at my-self, I see a body ready to bear children: hips waiting, like saddles, to transport small humans. I see hints of an ancient plan calling me to comply. And because of these hints, I believe I am a descen-dant of the prairie women who roam in my imagination. I might have been made for the land. Yet, like the women before me, those who left their first homes to start a life on the prairie, I left my home for a life I could not have on the land.

At nineteen I told my mom that I am gay. The announcement happened over lunch at a dimly lit Village Inn. This was not how I planned to tell her, surrounded by the sticky chewing of senior citizens, sawing into a piece of rubbery lasagna. But for some reason the truth came out after she prompted me to tell her what was going on. I wasn't myself, she said. Wasn't happy. Hadn't been the same since I'd left for college. She was right. When I told her that, indeed, something wasn't quite right, she started to ask—with a wince on her face—if I was having sex with boys now, if I was pregnant, or if I was doing drugs. Her list was almost funny to me, as none of those problems was relevant or seemed remotely possible. My true issue was probably the furthest from her mind, the most improbable of all of scenarios.

"No, Ma. I'm— I'm—" And at that moment something pro-pelled me to put a word to a feeling I'd never before named. "I'm a lesbian." As soon as my mom heard this, she enunciated my name the way she did when I was goofing off and she didn't find it funny anymore.

"Mel-an-ie, you are not a lesbian." It was as if the word lesbian had been packaged, shipped from Japan, and delivered to her doorstep without instructions. The way she said the word made me feel uncomfortable and sick. I was suddenly different, set apart.

Over the next few months she treated me like I had just been released from the hospital and she needed to be extra careful so as to not disturb my wound. She spoke in an upbeat tone, asking me how things were going. And soon, after her initial shock and denial, she became amazingly supportive, telling me that both she and my dad loved me no matter what. She even tried to engage in conversations about this newly open aspect of my life. "So, now, what is this dance you are going to tonight? Oh, a gay dance with other gay kids? How nice."

When she spoke, my entire suite of internal organs flipped. I was not ready to be exposed. My secret was like an animal being transported to the vet, the dog or cat that has clawed at the pet carrier the entire time, wanting out, but when finally there and released, runs, scared, back to the safety of the tiny prison. After clawing for nineteen years, I had finally been released, but I wanted back in. I wanted safety. Conversations with my mom were awkward and uncomfortable. We didn't know how to talk about something that was never supposed to be, something that never before had emerged on the prairie we knew. And so with the passage of time we simply stopped talking.

While I'm not certain she told anyone aside from my dad, Mom likely delivered the news to my siblings over time, like slipping them sour baby aspirin tablets. Because we all didn't talk about it together, being gay became my mental headline when I returned home. I couldn't stop thinking about it. I went to the bathroom: *I'm gay.* I opened the microwave: *I'm gay.* I answered the phone: *I'm gay.* My family and I concentrated on everything in the periphery of my life, spending an obscene amount of time talking about my job, my house, and my travels—but never really my life. And when I was home during those years, the TV, which was always on too loud, without fail ran a special on someone or something gay, and we would all freeze. None of us wanted to acknowledge the obvious discomfort and change the channel. Instead, we'd start looking out the window at the corn, as if we could suddenly see it growing. All the while I was screaming *I'm gay!* in my head, like a crazy person.

Four years later, at age twenty-three, I decided to try to break the silence again. I went home determined to talk with my mom about a breakup with a girlfriend. Though I had hidden the entire relationship from Mom —from everyone—the pain of separation stunned me in a way that made action necessary. I had exhausted all of the resources in my immediate life. My friends had said everything they were supposed to say. I had paid a therapist to help me visualize my ex-girlfriend as a soft, rotting peach, in order to make our parting easier. I had turned to the God of my childhood. Nothing had worked. Finally, although my mom and I had for years avoided the topic of me being gay, I was determined to apply her love to my real wounds for once. I was going to expose my secret. I was going to open up again.

Before we broke up, my girlfriend, whom I had introduced to my parents and often brought home as a friend, could not understand why, after having already confessed to my mom, I would not talk with her about my life. "You are being totally ridiculous," she would say. "They know about us. How can they not know? You just need to talk to them."

"It just takes too much energy," I would reply. What I meant, however, was that it took too much energy to explain to my girlfriend why both my family and I carried around the burden of silence, why it was too hard to reopen a conversation that was comfortably shut, a reality that was present but just lacked language. "Yes, I'm sure they know that we're together. So why does it matter?" I'd continue, frustrated because she couldn't understand.

At that point she would look at me and respond, "Because your silence keeps you away from your home." This was true. I had stopped going home frequently, because avoiding the silence was easier than being within it, especially being a crazy person within it, unable to think of anything else.

When I got home for my big confession, I took a deep breath and walked into the house. "Mom?"

Mom called back instantly, emerging from the laundry room with a thread and needle in hand: "My baby girl is home!" Her voice fed the lonely ache in my belly.

"How was your ride home?" she asked as she gave me a hug.

"Good. Long."

"Did you stop?"

"Ah, yeah." I thought for a second as I started rummaging through the refrigerator. "Once. In Alexandria. I got some gas and water."

"You made good time then."

As Mom lingered in the laundry room I thought about how I could casually bring up the topic before Dad got home. I fumbled around with the words in my head. *Mom, I'm going through a really hard time right now. Mom, I need to talk.*

"Mom, when's Dad coming home?" I asked, as I peeked into the laundry room. It was as always: towels folded on the dryer, Dad's dirty work clothes piled on the floor, Mom's sewing projects laid out by her sewing machine, and the second refrigerator—stocked with frozen hamburger—humming in the corner.

"He's already been home for dinner, so he probably won't be back until supper," she said.

I kicked piles of clothes out of my way and walked over to the sewing machine. "Okay, let's go for a walk soon," I said, and leaned over to where my mom sat, to give her another short hug. "I've been in the car all morning." Relieved, I knew I had the time to muster up the strength to talk.

Mom and I always take long walks when I go home. Our typical route is four miles long: two miles down a gravel road and two miles down a dirt road. A walk, I thought, would be a perfect place to bring up my life, to share my pain.

"Ready?" Mom had bundled herself in random clothes from the closet, including my old maroon letterman's jacket and a green Pioneer stocking cap—the clothing equivalent of a hot dish. I smiled at the reality that no one would see us and grabbed a green hat for myself.

We walked, *crunch, crunch,* our steps loud on the gravel, methodical, relaxing. We walked for a mile, maybe two. We talked about my siblings, my job, the latest news from my classmates, my house. I was half listening, half rehearsing. *Mom, I know we haven't talked for years, but I really need you. Mom, I've been crying a lot lately. Mom, do you and Dad ever talk about what's going on in my life?*

"Mom," I blurted out, obviously interrupting her, though I had no idea what she was saying.

"Yes?" she asked. I stopped. The pain planted itself in my throat, restricting my breathing and my tears, limiting my ability to wrap my vocal cords around the words that tried to make their way from my tired head. Silence. I watched the clouds move above the fields, dark gray with a rare deep green, creating the illusion of depth and texture. A late autumn rain was near. *How beautiful,* I thought to myself. In that moment I was so moved by the clouds, by their freedom, that I felt a small tunnel open within me. Tears started brimming in my eyes and I tried to hide them.

"What? What's the matter?" Mom asked, worried.

I looked at my mom in her green stocking cap. She was the most unassuming vision in the world at that moment: a woman in the Homemakers and Craft Club, who decorated her kitchen with images of chickens, and who made me—her vegetarian daughter—lasagna alongside steak suppers just because she loved me. Here we were, on the edge of North Dakota, surrounded by the silence of my childhood, and I could not speak.

"What is it, honey?" Mom asked again.

As quickly as it had opened, the tunnel in my throat closed. I looked up, looked past Mom, looked down the long road. The silence, the emptiness, the openness around us was too big for me to fill. "Nothing," I said, swallowing my story in the same way I had for years. Mom and I both continued walking—crunching the silence away.

I did not know then that the power of silence would be a force like none other in our lives—and that the words would not leave me for another seven years.

Can I mark a *precise* beginning with my mom, my dad, my family, our silence? If life resembles a river—the Mississippi perhaps—flowing through land, bumping into cities, carrying commerce, with tributaries feeding the drama every few miles, there is a beginning: a small spot in Minnesota. This beginning spot in the world is a simple natural part of the earth; it is marked with a proud wooden sign and sits about halfway between my home in Minneapolis and my childhood home in North Dakota. Yes, even the Mississippi has a beginning.

In a tree near the little green house is where the story of my silence begins, the first trickle. The story that will mark me as different, that will call for me to make a covenant with my soul to keep a secret from my family in order to protect them from something that was not supposed to be in North Dakota. It is the story that will cause me to step back and observe people, catch them looking to the horizon, settling into their thoughts, ignoring the conversation around them, only to snap back, their temporary absence unnoticed—except by me.

The beginning: I am in the tree. At the base of the tree several trunks come out of the earth and reach into the sky, creating a palm for my small body. I am wearing knit mittens, which easily catch on tree knobs.

I am too young to grasp concepts of God, or creation, or even nothingness. I only know that I'm living, sitting in a tree, with little blue mittens, a red scarf, an orange winter coat, and the awareness that I, simply, *am*. And I experience in this tree, on this winter day, my first craving to love completely. Before the definitions, before the kisses with boys, before the Bible verses and college talks, before the fear of my family and the small-town silence, before everything, the prairie delivered the knowledge that I would, for whatever reason, love a woman.

What would life have been like had I run inside to share this moment with my mom? How might life have evolved from that point? That sort of story is impossible to know because somewhere in my four-year-old consciousness I already knew silence. Because I did not share my awareness with anyone on that winter day, my entire childhood will pass with the quiet prairie as my only witness.

Harvest Retreat

"I'm coming home for harvest," I say to Mom, as if returning for harvest is the most natural thing in the world and something I do routinely.

"Why?" She is on the other end of the phone. I hear Dad and the TV in the background.

"I've just decided I want a break. Thought I could drive truck. See if I like farming."

"Well, you *won't* like farming. What about your job?"

"I'm taking two weeks off. And, who knows, maybe I'll take a leave of absence. If not, I can work from the farm for the rest of the time."

"You won't like farming," she repeats. Here's a memory she may be considering: me, a seventh grader, whining when asked to mow the lawn.

"You don't know that."

"Yes, I do," she says, not finding it the least bit necessary to argue her case. Now I actually do feel like a kid again, having one of my arms-crossed, pouting tantrums, where Mom pats me on the cheek, and says, "Yes, dear, whatever you say."

Over the years Mom has told me I would not like farming, that I would go crazy living in the middle of nowhere. She's said this even though during the summers when we yipped at Mom's heels like restless puppies, wanting to do something beyond riding our bikes to the Holtz kids' farm, Mom assured us we were not missing any big whoop in town. I now understand that *she* likely was the one who wanted to run to civilization, away from a life where she had to mow a lawn the size of a football field, clean a house that couldn't hold out the farm dirt, drive thirty miles for groceries, and brave treacherous country winter roads. Yes, she wanted to run back to civilization, even if her version of civilization—her hometown, Wahpeton, population 8,500— would hardly be considered a metropolitan hub of activity to most people.

I fully realized Mom wasn't all that fond of farm life a couple of years before my decision to go home for harvest. Mom called out of the blue to announce that she and Dad were moving to Wahpeton, which is thirty miles from the farm. I was shocked. This news came at the same time Donny announced he was getting married. Donny's proposal to Julia was his step into the land of adulthood, and Mom's opportunity to step back into the land of people. From Mom's perspective, this was the unfolding of the natural order, just like when Mom was whisked onto the farm at twenty-one. Dad wouldn't retire but would slowly hand things over to Donny, like my grandpa had to Dad and my uncle. Letting Donny move into the farmhouse was the first step.

Without warning, Mom called and rattled off details about houses she and Dad were looking at in Wahpeton. What did I think about this floor plan versus that one? What about light-colored carpet, would it get dirty? This house doesn't have a fire-place, but that's not really necessary, right?

Wait, wait. What? I shook my head like a cartoon character flattened by falling off of a cliff, who now needed to inflate my body, starting with my head.

My parents' move marked the end of one era and the begin-ning of another. I imagined a triangle: the farm is at one point, Wyndmere is another, and Barney, population eighty, is the third. Each point is eight miles apart. My dad has spent his entire life within this triangle. He was raised on the land, the oldest of four kids, like me. He went to school in Wyndmere, the same town where later as an adult he served on the school board and hauled his carload of kids to Anderson's Café on Sunday mornings after church for "family style," which was endless servings of potatoes, gravy, chicken, ham, corn, and white buns. He's spent years driving through Barney, often dropping by the bar on his way home to converse with other farmers.

When I considered how things should be in this world, on this planet, I thought that naturally Dad should remain within this triangle of land where he belonged. He had never lived in a town and I couldn't picture him in one, not even a tiny one. To be fair, it's not like my dad is some forest animal, like we don't let him go out in public, into the rest of the world. No. Mom and Dad frequently venture into Fargo to shop, they visit me in Minneapolis, and they've taken trips to places like Alaska and Hawaii. But even within their mobility there has always been a boomerang force that returned Dad to his La-Z-Boy on the farm. But not anymore, and I've never witnessed my mom in such bliss.

Since they've moved to Wahpeton, Mom has trumpeted her liberation. She no longer has to plan her grocery lists, or haul her sewing supplies to sew with the Material Girls, or drive for thirty minutes just to meet with her Under Cover book club, or worry about the roads on snowy days. She is home.

But *my* home has changed.

"Here. Talk to your father," Mom says, and hands me off to Dad.

"Hello?" Dad's voice is on the line now.

"Dad, hi. Can I work for you over harvest?"

Pause.

"I don't know. What would you do?"

"Drive a truck," I say, like it should make immediate sense to him.

"Oh," he says.

Another pause.

"Don't you think I'm capable?"

"I don't know."

"You don't know?" I'm not particularly pleased by his lack of enthusiasm. "Well, I'll just hang out then. Follow you."

"When?"

"Um, September? October?" I realize not knowing exactly when one should be home for harvest is a bit of a handicap. I know it is approximately August through November, depending upon the year.

"Where will you stay?"

"I don't know. I guess I'll just go back and forth. Crash at the farm with Donny and Julia. Stay with you and Ma for part of the time. We can commute to the farm together!"

"Okay, sweetie," he says, placating me. Dad is a man of few words, so I didn't expect to have much of a dialogue. But in this moment I want him to take me seriously.

Several weeks before I made the call to Mom and Dad, I scribbled a mantra and taped it to my computer, as if I'm some sort of mediation guru:

> *One thing at a time.*
> *As devotion.*
> *As prayer.*

I've changed jobs in the years since Melissa and I spoke about returning to the farm. I now lead a team in a marketing department and mostly work from home. I start my days by strapping a headset on, situating myself at my desk, and dialing into the first of several daily conference calls. Shortly after the calls begin, the e-mails start. I try to pick them off one by one, but soon they begin to pile up, like the Tetris game when you've lost control because you can't organize the blocks falling from the top of the screen. Next my instant messenger chimes with colleagues around the country pinging me, as we say. At any given point during the day I might be on the phone with ten people and simultaneously carrying on conversations with a subset of the same people via IM, all the while trying to catch up on e-mail. And I haven't yet tackled the projects—the actual work—that must be done in the meantime.

Ten hours later, twelve hours later, fourteen hours later, my body is in contortions: stabbing pain in my neck, in my arms, in my back, in my tailbone. Fourteen hours later, done with work. *Done with work?*

When the mantra poured out of me, I was standing at my second-story window, coffee in hand, about to grab my headset. The sun was rising in the distance behind a church steeple; a bit of morning fog still lingered in the treetops. I noticed dew on the branches and heard the birds chirping their carefree morning hymns. I was about to shut the beauty down, shut the stillness down, about to jump on the phone to engage in my jaw-clenching, shoulder-tightening habitual ritual, when I realized, quite plainly, my multitasking was a poison. *I might as well take a knife and stab it into my shoulder*, I thought. So I grabbed a piece of paper and wrote the mantra to help me remember to care for myself as diligently as if tending to a holy practice. The mantra worked—for a week.

Did I mention that I have a great job? That I work for a non-profit whose mission I believe in? An organization that actually lives by, breathes, and acts on its core values? A job where I work with brilliant, passionate, non-petty people?

The problem, the "gotcha," is that somewhere along the way I lost sight of *my* limits, of *my* passions, of *my* core values. In my great job I am possessed by perfection, by keeping up with my workload, by impressing my colleagues, by doing more. So even though I have a great job, I think when one wanders from the center of who one is, the universe will take even the most dazzling situation and concoct an ultimatum, an impetus for change. My impetus was my body rebelling. My piercing pains were whispering, *You need to step back, take a break, take inventory.*

I knew I needed a break, but a regular vacation did not seem radical enough. Any other year I would have plotted a trip to another part of the world, hightailed it to a restful place by the ocean, or found a cabin where I would stoke a fire and do little beyond planning meals to accompany my daily coffee and wine consumption. And I considered several possibilities for this year: another trip to Italy, check out Thailand, hit Bali, venture to Greece. And there were some breathtaking national parks I hadn't explored yet, places where, if the world had been created on an assembly line, you'd figure the workers forgot to pay attention, allowing the earth to bubble into spectacular anomalies. But I couldn't shake my conversation with Melissa about returning home, finding a small plot of land, driving a grain truck.

It was time.

I was not so naive to think farming is less stressful than my job. In fact, I was certain that life on the farm would be exponentially more taxing. My dad probably carries the weight of the world when he deals with uncontrollable factors like the weather and the grain market. Still, the truck and the AM radio and the grain elevator and the gravel roads and the small-town bars and open sky were, at least right then, attractive. What would it be like to be my own boss? To spend my days with the land, rather than a computer? To linger on stillness and beauty, rather than shut it down?

And there was something else: my growing disconnect with people. I've never been able to feel at home in the city. Maybe this is because, on the prairie, people's close connections extend beyond blood relatives. And where blood is concerned, families plug into each other's lives in multiple ways, like Tinker Toys. In my family alone, some serious small-town connections have manifested. My Grandpa Hoffert and his brother married sisters. A good friend of mine from high school married my aunt's brother. My cousin from a neighboring town married the sister of a girl in my class. Another uncle married my high school friend's aunt.

"That explains a lot," my partner Nancy will say, teasing me, listening for the cousin intermarriage story as a clue to why I am accident-prone. She was raised in a Minneapolis suburb and thinks my connection to people from back home is peculiar.

If I run into someone from North Dakota I don't know, chances are we will find a connection by rattling off last names and small towns, like drilling in on a Google map where the world zooms by and you land on a specific spot on the earth. I feel grounded after these encounters—accounted for, in a weird way.

My sense of disconnect from people in the city is not new, but I've suppressed it over time. When I arrived at college I was simultaneously intrigued and disorientated by the flood of people. College was a sort of people department store. I was dazzled by the plethora of options, having lived in a people mini-mart my entire life. Yet I was unsure how to navigate this new world of strange faces.

When my dorm emptied on game days I couldn't understand why anyone would care about a game if they hadn't known the players their entire lives. Filling the bleachers with hundreds of virtual strangers felt somehow insincere. I know my trepidation was likely a bit strange, given our cultural worship of athletes we don't know personally. But when it came to the college players, I couldn't even attach celebrity to them, so I couldn't make the game, the crowd, the players matter.

At the time I even liked football. I had spent my entire life going to Friday-night football games where floodlights illuminated the grain elevators on the edge of town. The whole town came to the games too, taking their respective places. My friend's dad parked his red pick-up on the opposing team's side to get a good view. Some parents ran along the sidelines like chimps at a zoo follow visitors with peanuts. Other parents lined the metal bleachers. When the whistles blew they'd crank their necks to peek at the football game being played by the elementary school kids behind the risers. Recent high school grads stashed their pickup tailgates with beer; by the end of the night the guys would be jumping on each other like warriors from a lost tribe. Popcorn scent from the concession stand lurked in the chilly air, seducing the crowd. And everyone had what I dare say resembled a collective orgasm at each interception and touchdown.

This was my life. Yet as the years tick by and farms are consolidated and people migrate to bigger towns, this web of connection will stretch, will thin, will dissolve. People won't experience an extended family, like mine, that stretches beyond blood and into the land.

A few days after I called my parents to announce my harvest plan, one of my gay husbands, Ryan, picked me up for dinner. My gay husbands, affectionately nicknamed, are two dear friends, Ryan and Montana, a couple who incessantly fight but are perfectly matched with a passion for antiques, architecture, and working on their house with the attention to detail of skilled—no, obsessed—glass etchers. They, along with a handful of other good friends, are the closest I have gotten to a sense of community in the city.

Ryan is sarcastic and witty, skinny, and eternally dramatic about hating his life and losing his hair. He'll have nothing to do with my assurances—while he's pressing the hair on his forehead back, showing me his hairline—that he has more hair than me. Montana is grounded, sensitive; he has the rough handsomeness of a cowboy, balanced by artistic sensibilities and musical talent. He'll spend hours in the basement stripping and refinishing found treasures to a stunning brilliance.

"Monta-NA, it did not happen that way," Ryan will jump in when Montana talks, refining story details to his point of view.

"Rude! Let me finish," Montana will respond, looking at me with an exasperated expression that says, *Can you believe him?* as if this pattern hasn't transpired hundreds of times over dinner. They are like two crabs in a bucket, crawling over each other for airtime.

—m—

"Woman!" Ryan gets out of his car and breezes past me, rounding the side of my house to investigate. "Good lord, woman, you have *got* to trim your bushes." He stops and looks me up and down disapprovingly to make sure I catch the double entendre.

My bushes are a bit unruly, this is true. They are covering my windows and reaching up to my eaves. But who has the time?

Next Ryan runs to the back corner of the house, stops at another overgrown green thing, gasps, and covers his lips with his hand, as if he has spotted the Devil himself.

"Do you know what this is? *Honey*, this is a tree. Do you understand me? A tree!"

I shrug, *I guess.*

"You have *got* to dig the roots out. Immediately. It will continue to grow and will absolutely ruin your foundation." Ryan has called the tree out several times, though he always comes upon it as if he's discovered it anew.

"I don't have time! I'm too busy," I state my weak case.

"Pah-*lease*." Ryan rolls his eyes and continues his inspection of my house, walking quickly around the perimeter, bending over every few feet to tug at a weed. As he performs his inspection, he simultaneously lectures me on how I have nothing to complain about and how unbelievably busy he and Montana are: torturously melting the exterior paint off of their house with a heat gun ("You have no idea how hard it is, we can only do about three square feet in a weekend"); waking at dawn to tend to the yard ("Woman, I get up at the crack to water every single plant, every day; look at your poor neglected plants"); refinishing this, scraping that ("You must keep up on this stuff, honey"). And on and on and on.

"You know nothing about being busy," he shakes his head, completing his rant. Then he looks around, lowers his voice, and says, "What do you think the neighbors think of these crazy bushes?"

"I'm sure they don't care or notice," I say. "Plus, I don't really know any of them anyway." I push him toward the car. "Come. Let's eat."

Over an Indian dinner of naan, rice, and red-brown curry dishes, Ryan and I catch up on life. Montana, who works at an ad agency, is in New York on a photo shoot, so Ryan is in rare form: free and relaxed.

"Oh, my God, let's go to Italy this fall," Ryan says midway through our meal. "I haven't taken a serious vacation in years. It would be a dream."

I take a sip of my wine to wash down a bite of my mattar paneer, preparing to broach the subject of how Italy may have to wait since I am, well, vacationing in North Dakota this year. As my pseudo husbands, these two have no shortage of opinions about what I should do with my life. And so I am not sure how Ryan will react to my plan.

"I would absolutely love to. But, ah, I'm not sure if I can this year." I chew slowly and continue. "You know. I've been thinking a lot about whether I could live in North Dakota?"

"What do you mean, *live?*" Ryan is already looking at me with a familiar, disapproving scowl.

"I don't know. Sometimes I crave getting away. Living in a small town." I know that in some way, Ryan understands my impulse to move. His vision of reprieve just happens to be slightly different than mine: a small apartment in Manhattan with no yard, no maintenance, no square feet to refurbish.

"No," Ryan winces, "not North Dakota, for Christ's sake." Then his eyes light up. "Look, if you're going to move to a small town, why not go someplace pretty?" Okay, so he is not *totally* putting the kibosh on my idea of getting away. "What about Portland. Don't all the lesbos like Portland?"

"Well, yes, Portland is gorgeous, but it isn't that small."

Ryan's brow scrunches. Before he can respond I jump in, "Anyway, I'm not sure about Italy. At the very least I'm thinking of taking my vacation on the farm this year. I want to hang out for harvest, visit small towns, figure out what I should do next." I sigh. "Plus, you know I've always wanted to be a real, full-time writer. After a day of work it is impossible to sit at the computer one minute longer. With a month off I could work on the farm and also make time to write."

Ryan's rubs his chin. He looks at me thoughtfully and nods.

"It will be an adventure, Ry," I say, persuading him. "I've never been back to the farm for more than a week, if that long."

"Well, we'll see how this goes," he says. His consideration of my words is almost gracious for someone who usually manages my life.

The next morning I get up, brew coffee, and compose an e-mail to my boss. Though I can barely imagine letting go, imagine my job going on without me, imagine what my colleagues might think, I request a month off to return to the farm for harvest.

When Love Gains a Face

In seventh grade I drew my first love to me by confessing that I had seen a penis—a real, live penis, gray in color and shaped like a polish sausage that had been slightly bent in the middle, as if squashed by a milk carton while lying in the grocery bag.

"Did you *touch* it?" Jessica screamed, sitting on my parents' brown couch in our basement next to my friend Sarah. The three of us had buried the coffee table with enough Doritos, Mountain Dew, and Tombstone Pizza to feed us well into the night. We planned to stay awake until midnight to watch *Friday Night Videos*. Sarah and I had to explain to Jessica what *Friday Night Videos* was, that at midnight we could watch Madonna, Michael Jackson, and Wham! on TV, singing all of our favorite songs. This was before satellite TV dishes were possible on the farm, before we knew that there was such a thing as MTV and VH1.

Jessica had never watched *Friday Night Videos*, and this, in my opinion, was strange. What was even stranger was that when we explained the magic of *Friday Night Videos*, she just shrugged, saying, "Okay, whatever, I'll watch."

My confession about a penis sighting was another thing. Once I launched into my story, sharing secrets to pass the time until midnight, Jessica's eyes grew wide. She was attentive, sitting at the edge of the couch, ready to interview me as if I was some kind of superstar like Madonna.

"You have *got* to tell us," she repeated, "did you *touch* it?"

"No. I didn't touch it. But—"

I put my finger into the air, signaling a pause. I had an audience and was going to make the most of it. I placed the Mountain

43

Dew to my lips and took a long gulp in an effort to draw out my story, which tortured the two girls sitting on the brown couch.

"But what?" they said in unison.

"But," I repeated and stared at them from across the littered coffee table. I was like a traveling salesman with the townspeople gathered around me to buy my healing potions. I placed my Mountain Dew on the coffee table and situated myself in the La-Z-Boy.

"But—*he* touched it!" I threw my head into a pillow and let out a loud scream. Jessica and Sarah screamed too, at the top of their lungs. I shushed them, signaling upstairs to where my parents were already in bed.

"It was sticking out in front of him like a popsicle. Dangling," I said in a lowered voice.

Jessica wrinkled her nose in disbelief. "That is so disgusting! What was he *thinking*?"

"Dis-gus-ting." I repeated Jessica's words, curling my own nose, pleased that she was interested in my story.

"I can't believe he showed it to you. What did you say?" Jessica asked.

"I asked him if he needed mustard," I lied to make her laugh. The truth was that when Mark Tron called me to the science table in seventh grade to show me his penis, I didn't know what to say. When I got to the table I stood on my tiptoes and peered to the other side where he was sitting, stroking the sausage with an ill expression on his face. I simply looked at him and considered the body part I didn't have.

I had known Jessica my entire life, though we did not become friends until junior high. In fact, in elementary school she bothered me immensely. She popped into the world polished and evolved, not having to muddle through the messiness of adolescence the way most everyone else does. In some regards she had the eerie, adult-like posturing of a well-trained child model. When she over-articulated her words, as if she was copying a news reporter on TV, I cringed with embarrassment for her. She was fiercely competitive and quick to correct anyone who was wrong, even her teachers. And when she wanted to be the best, she always was. She was promoted to the sixth-grade basketball team when she was in fifth. She sang solos at all of the elementary concerts because her voice was as clear and powerful as a professional singer's. She took first place in every event on track and field day. She got straight As in every subject. And, on top of it all, her face was perfectly symmetrical. She had a bright, wide smile, a square jaw, full lips, and shiny, dark hair.

Watching Jessica was like chewing on tinfoil. Sometimes I was jealous of her because, while she acted as an adult, I had always felt like an adult myself. Sometimes I was annoyed, watching her navigate the world with what seemed to be an unfair amount of privilege. And sometimes I was just downright uncomfortable, watching the little anomaly belt out solos while closing her eyes and rocking back and forth. This was not how we were taught to act in small-town North Dakota.

When we entered junior high, my irritation toward Jessica turned into curiosity. This all happened, oddly enough, during junior high band practice. From where I sat next to the trombones and below the drums, I had a clear view of Jessica and her trumpet.

Our conductor was a man who I assumed had never lived in a small town. He was round, with a small mustache, and always had classical music playing in his office. Looking back I think it must have been his love of music, not of children, that led him to his job in the middle of nowhere. He perspired profusely while he clicked his tongue and waved his arm in the air, enunciating his words as if to beg the band to mimic his staccato perfection. "Not good enough, ladies and gentlemen. Sssstart over. From. The. Top."

While he labored to achieve a symphonic performance from a clunky junior high band, the rest of us—not sharing his love—found third period the perfect time to conduct junior high business under his blind rule. Love notes floated from the flutes to the drummers. The drummers sailed spitballs at the saxophones. And I watched Jessica.

Jessica, like our conductor, was blind to the activity around her. While he labored to get the flutes to flutter, and while the rest of the band buzzed in misbehavior, Jessica studied her music and played her trumpet silently. I watched her fingers repeat the notes over and over again. When the conductor released the flutes and moved to the trumpets, Jessica sat at the edge of her chair—ready.

"Okay, ladies and gentlemen, let's hear it! Ta, ta," he led the trumpets into their part. The trumpets fell out of the melody, one by one, not able to keep up, until at last only Jessica remained and finished the part effortlessly. When the stanza was over, the conductor pointed his wand at Jessica.

"Jessica. Play!" Jessica put the trumpet to her lips, sat on the tip of her chair with her back straight, tapped her foot, and played. "Now, the rest of you. See? The rhythm goes *Ta, Ta-ta, Ta.* Not *Ta. Ta. Ta. Ta.*" The boys ran their hands through their oily hair, frustrated because they couldn't get the part right. And Jessica slipped to the back of her chair and relaxed for the first time all period.

An odd thing happened to me when Jessica put the instrument to her lips. Her perfectly crafted notes traveled through the air and seemed to settle into the cavities of my body, swirling in the open space between my ribs, winding around my lungs until I felt weak. It was as if the meat of my bones separated from my ribcage, leaving me open and hollow. I was jealous, no doubt—Jessica yet again set apart—but there was also more. I was stunned, almost, by her perfection. While I watched her day after day in band, I yearned to understand her drive and sense of purpose.

The more I watched her—content in her own world, working toward some greater goal the rest of us couldn't see—the more I wondered if she might be the one who could understand me. Maybe this strange girl looked up to the sky and daydreamed of the possibility of deeper connections. Maybe she, on her farm—which was sixteen miles from mine, separated by Wyndmere, two sets of railroad tracks, a long stretch of highway and several gravel roads—felt the breeze on her face and knew that there was a different reality? A different way to love?

One morning when the conductor called on us, the alto clarinets, I decided—as I put my reed to my lips and looked into his sweaty pits for a nod of approval—that I would no longer be jealous of Jessica. She would now become my friend. Soon after, as if perfectly orchestrated by me setting my goal, my friend Sarah, who was in Jessica's grade, invited Jessica to our *Friday Night Videos* sleepover at my house.

Jessica's and my friendship began slowly, but then it became absolute, like a body organ we just realized we needed in order to live. For me, our friendship was an evolution past the small town and everything I knew. For her, our friendship was a window into the small town and the incomprehensible social life of her peers. For the next six years we spent days and nights side by side. We were not always alone—there were the others, our friends. For thirteen years, all of us—twenty-one in my grade, sixteen in hers—were together from the time the first bell rang until late into the evening. After school the gym echoed with squeaky shoes and bouncing balls from some practice or another. The band room rang with band or choir groups. Kids hung in the library practicing for speech competitions. Small towns, I now realize, call for kids to diversify in ways larger towns would never imagine.

At the time we became friends, Jessica had not kissed any boys, and she had certainly not seen one of their penises. To her, boys were ridiculously underdeveloped creatures with whom she could be friends but whose kisses would be the equivalent of kissing her brother. I, on the other hand, was *experienced*. I had kissed enough boys in our small town to give her a play-by-play of what it was like to have one of them stick his wet tongue in my mouth.

When we started to spend more time together, I filled the one information void in Jessica's life where she was not yet an expert: the world of guys.

"Imagine sucking on an overgrown slug. That's about what it is like to kiss Josh Cunningham," I said, feeling good that I could be an expert in something. She usually looked at me with a half-raised eyebrow.

"Do you think you're a slut?" she asked me one night, not judging but earnestly wanting to know what might qualify someone as a slut.

After seriously pondering her question for a few seconds, I responded, "Nah. I won't have sex until I'm married."

Sex was out of the question. Sex was a sin, as far as I was concerned. Worse, it was one of those sins that put your soul in serious trouble, according to what I had learned about the Ten Commandments.

"I won't have sex before I'm married either," Jessica said. "No way."

Jessica took me on like a sort of intern, imparting to me her worldly experience which otherwise would have been quite useless in her farmhouse surrounded by little more than miles of open pasture.

"This is what you need," she said as she laid out her new underwear collection in front of me while I sat on her bed doing homework. "Enough of your cotton Hanes Her Way—no more," she lectured as she unpacked bras and panties from tissue. "Feel this bra. Just like silk."

I couldn't understand, for the life of me, what could possibly make one bra better or worse than another. But Jessica's knowledge gave life to dormant objects that I had not yet noticed. Bras and panties became items with texture and color. Baking had a process and a science. Sports teams had important heroes and losers. Jessica had a sort of magic wand. She would focus on something, extend her wand, and all of a sudden something I had never noticed or thought about had a place in my mind.

Jessica collected her knowledge by doing and experiencing. In the summer she spent her days outside planting flowers, weeding gardens, checking on and feeding cattle, and mowing the grass. In the winter she baked with her mom, making pies and testing recipes she always wanted me to try. While she was out working I was at my farm, watching *The Facts of Life* and *Diff'rent Strokes*, not as eager to help my parents.

When Jessica turned fourteen, old enough to drive in North Dakota, we escaped to the movies in Wahpeton. Movies did for Jessica what she did for me—they introduced her to new perspectives, other worlds, adventure and drama. She was drawn into the stories, so that for weeks after we saw a movie she would research the movie's topic and sing the soundtrack at the top of her lungs. Jessica also bought books on whatever the movie was about. Then for weeks after that she rattled off facts, recited history, and speculated about the movie characters until she was practically an expert on whatever had triggered her interest, whether the details of World War II, the vegetation of Africa, or the mechanics of ocean tides. "You are like a walking encyclopedia—it's not normal," I made fun of her, feeding her ego while she fed my desire to experience the depth of the world.

At this time I had daydreams about love. The images that flooded my mind were more like poetry than full stories, with their abbreviated thoughts and stanzas of emotion. I imagined fields of wheat, sunshine, forts, tall grass, and a knowing person by my side. And this sense of *knowingness* was the key, because while the picture was never quite clear, the love I imagined was not about sex but about a connection that somehow transcended sex. This love was like the deepest and most-known comforts of the world. Clean sheets. A favorite blanket. A kitchen with warm bread. The desire that rose in my chest during these faraway thoughts was a contrast to the emptiness that settled upon me on hot summer nights, when the farm boys scampered around me like blind baby mice, looking for a place to settle their sticky lips. And while my daydreams were neither right nor wrong, as the tone of my voice was neither right nor wrong, I kept my desires a secret because the person by my side always happened to be a woman.

Then, one day, for the first time, while chewing my pencil and ignoring math in favor of these thoughts, my mental poetry had a face. I saw Jessica.

On our first sleepover Jessica could not get into *Friday Night Videos*, but she was eternally curious about what sort of junior high drama she had missed.

"Okay. You two need to tell me every single boy you have kissed. List them out. One by one. And don't miss anyone." Jessica grabbed the bag of Doritos and wrapped herself in a blanket.

Sarah thought about her list for a minute. "Okay. I'll tell you." She looked at Jessica, setting the rules. "But you can't tell anyone."

"I won't!"

"I've made out with Bill, Charlie, and Doug." Sarah said, holding up a finger for each one. Doug was her latest. They had been going together for two weeks.

"Everyone has kissed Bill and Charlie," I chimed in.

"*You've* kissed them too?" Jessica looked at me with wide eyes.

"Yes, Charlie was my first kiss. A couple of years ago."

"I was there," Sarah joined. "We met them after Bible school. In the trees by the railroad tracks."

We had planned our meeting all week, poking the boys over the pews. At the end of our last day, we told our parents we were going to stay late to hang out with our friends at the Uptown Café. Instead we went to the edge of town—where the pavement turned to gravel—crossed over a set of railroad tracks, and snuck into a grove of trees. The boys pulled up on their bikes. Sticks crackled under our step as we made our way into the tiny forest.

The four of us sat in a matted area that had either been the resting place of deer or previously inhabited by other kids who had met in "the trees." With one boy facing one girl in the soft grass nest, we all closed our eyes, leaned in, and touched lips with a quick pucker. Charlie's soft lips touched mine and it was over. I opened my eyes and studied his freckles, wide lips, and white-blond hair.

"But that was, like, in fifth grade. Nothing. Innocent." I looked at Sarah. "The boys are all hands now. Making out with them is like wrestling an octopus," I said.

"I can't believe you guys have made out with Bill and Charlie," Jessica said. I think she might have been putting it all together, reconsidering the boys who had become her good friends. Reconsidering what we were all doing while she was studying. "Is it weird?"

"Well. Not weird. Though at first touching tongues is sort of strange," Sarah admitted to Jessica. I agreed by nodding my head. Sarah turned toward Jessica and sat straight up, getting ready to do something I would have never in a million years have dared. "Stick out your tongue, I'll show you," she said, as if telling Jessica to close her eyes so that she could apply eye shadow for the first time. My heart stopped, though the two didn't seem to flinch.

"Seriously?" Jessica said, in a way that sounded as if she was thankful for the opportunity, a science experiment where she could gain understanding but wouldn't have to kiss a real-life boy herself to figure it out.

"Sure. Here." Sarah squared her body so that they were directly in front of each other. After they were aligned, Sarah stuck out her tongue part way, just so the tip showed. Jessica stuck hers out a little too, as if headed for a sour Popsicle. They inched closer together until they finally met. My tongue prickled.

"Weird!" Jessica pulled back. She had never done anything of the sort in her life. "That felt so strange!"

I was horrified. I couldn't imagine touching Sarah's tongue with mine, not even for the purpose of scientific investigation. I also knew that what Jessica felt was nothing like it would feel to kiss a boy.

"Let's try again," Jessica said, now taking control, more than just a willing participant. The two of them tried their experiment a few more times, touching, screaming, then falling on their sides laughing while I shushed them from the La-Z-Boy, reminding them of my parents upstairs.

Suddenly the phone rang. I grabbed it quickly, knowing it was not for my parents, not at this time of night. When the world was finally dark, the boys started to call from other farmsteads. The three of us looked at each other, as if having been caught. We all knew we were doing something that would not be shared with anyone else. Jessica and Sarah dropped away from each other to opposite ends of the couch.

"Hello?" The voice, as expected, was Sarah's boyfriend of two weeks, checking in.

"It's Doug," I said with my hand over the phone, my heart still beating wildly.

Sarah hopped off of the couch to sit closer to the phone. Jessica jumped off of the couch too and came to sit by me on the recliner.

"Hilarious," she whispered. We rocked back and forth while Sarah talked. The room had grown dark, illuminated by only the glow of the TV.

"It is none of your business what we are talking about or what we are doing," Sarah teased Doug. "You'll just have to find out someday."

"So, do you actually like making out with boys?" Jessica asked me, rocking the chair with her leg.

"Sure." Her nearness both comforted and made me uneasy.

"I just don't know if I could do it."

"You could."

Jessica took my hand at that moment. All of the hair on my body prickled. "I am not sure if I would French. I think I would want it to be sweet and soft."

Without saying another word, her hand moved slowly up my arm to my face. She gently touched my cheek. "This is what it would be like," she whispered. I could feel the heat of her lips before they met my neck. She kissed me gently, planting a line of tiny kisses along my neck. Her kisses were so soft, tentative, as if she was kissing tissue paper and applying too much pressure might tear it. She ended at my jaw. After a small pause, she kissed the corner of my mouth.

"Yes. That's how I would want it to be," she whispered in my ear. We continued rocking, listening to Sarah—now oblivious to us—flirt on the phone.

Rubbers and Nipples on the Farm

It is fall, harvest time. I am almost home. The fields clip by my window like an eight-millimeter film reel someone left running. There is no sound. After hours of interstate, I meander down gravel roads that divide North Dakota into a series of symmetrical square-mile sections.

On the last hour of my drive, barns replace strip malls and suburban cookie-cutter houses. Avenues or streets do not identify the roads that take me home. Instead roads are marked by the names of families who worked the land after their ancestors claimed it under the Homestead Act. There is Elmer's Section, George's Half, Stone's, Hudson's, Carlson's, the Home Quarter, the Church Quarter. The branding of these spaces stays, even after those for whom the land was named were removed by the farm crisis or the death of the family patriarch.

When I first get home, before I find my dad or my brother, I stroll around the edge of the farm. I walk to a plot of land filled with idle John Deere tractors, older models that have given their years. I used to drive these tractors, helping my dad and my uncle with the spring planting. While childhood memory often distorts images, making objects bigger than they actually are, it is not so with this machinery. Everything is gigantic, so unlike anything that makes its way down the road in urban America.

After visiting the machinery I walk on makeshift roads that weave between old buildings and grain bins until I find myself at the barn. Pigeons buzz past my head as I climb the stairs to the hayloft. Once there, I peer out of the chute that looks over the farm and into a vast open world.

This is my way of reentering, my way of becoming acclimated to this strange place. For a long time this land was my only reference for how I understood the world. Even so, I must always reenter.

The four-hour drive, though not a terribly long distance, takes me far from my current life. In the city I've learned that walking two blocks can transport one into a completely different world. Neighborhoods change quickly. If that scale of measurement can be applied to my journey home, I am in another galaxy. At the farm the sky is different. The air is different. Even the dirt is different. In the city mud acts as a flytrap for candy wrappers, gum wads, abandoned newspapers, and sticky pennies. At the farm, dirt is clean. Farm dirt is rich with smell, texture, and even taste. Here dirt swallows seeds and spits them back whole. I, too, need to be whole. I need to heal, which is why I'm home.

From the barn I look at the sky and smile. I'm here. I'm home. In a bit I'll go to the shop to say hi to Dad and Donny, then I'll drive to Mom and Dad's new house and get settled. Tomorrow I'll rise with the sun, jump in the pickup with Dad, and my month on the farm will begin.

Harvest retreat, day one. I'm standing at what looks like a wall of cubbies you'd find in a kindergarten classroom, except I'm in the shop, in a loft space over the office, staring at a mess of assorted parts and pieces. Nothing looks familiar, and I mean *nothing.* A talk show plays in the background from a clock radio bolted to the wall below. Dad is crouching in front of me, holding up a plastic thing the size of my fist that sort of resembles a bolt or a screw.

"This is a coupler." He reaches down and picks up another part. "And this is a nipple. And see here"—he grabs another part—"you have your male end, your female end, and they go together like this."

At this point I am trying to be mature. I am not the handiest person in the world, and know this anatomy talk is common vernacular. If I spent more time at Ace Hardware this lesson wouldn't even cause me to blink, but then he continues.

"See here, this rubber piece? This goes between these two parts." He's holding up what I later learn is an O-ring. "And these are clamps."

Clamps? I can't take it.

"Dad. What's with the nipples and rubbers and male and female parts? Good God."

Dad smirks. "That's life. Better get used to it."

He continues to point out parts scattered on the floor and caked with mud: barbed tees, 90-degree elbows, 45-degree elbows, reducers and reducer nipples, manifold fittings, plugs and caps, cam locks. Each time he picks something up and throws it into a cubby I look closely to try to distinguish it. But much of it looks the same. And several of these pieces are still, ah, coupled or screwed together, so he shows me how to use a vice to secure the combined pieces and a giant wrench to pull the pieces apart. The wrench is rusty, so he sprays it with WD-40 and hands it to me. I hesitate, assuming he's not thinking clearly, handing me the wrench covered with rust and slime, but then I remember I'm a farmer today and grab it.

My assignment is to take these parts and sort them all into the right cubbies, which are partially labeled, but mostly not. "What is all of this stuff used for?" I ask, wanting to know what my labor will accomplish.

"These are parts for the sprayer," Dad says, getting up.

I nod my head and look over the room. In addition to the piles of sprayer parts strewn on the floor, there are other things scattered everywhere in this messy eight-by-twelve space. And I don't mean "messy" like in a house. The space is messy with oil and dirt and mouse feces. The layer of thick dust makes me feel as if I am in a sepia-toned movie. And there is a strong smell of cat urine, much more potent than the whiffs of urine I pick up in the city.

—ɯ—

Just an hour before, I had filled my coffee cup with Folgers (the official coffee of the farm) and jumped into the pickup with Dad for our commute to the farm. The morning was foggy. The land is too wet to finish the bean harvest today, Dad told me, so the combines will not be going out. Our work will be in the shop.

On the drive I studied my dad. I could still see him from my four-year-old vantage point: handsome and boyish, like men in magazines from the seventies, with shaggy hair, white-toothed smiles, sitting on ski slopes with a drink in one hand and a ciga-rette in another. Today his beard—which he usually has this time of year, no time to shave—is almost all white. He's wearing his Lee stretch jeans. And his hands are like small coconuts, thick and meaty, permanently scarred and browned with tractor oil. His right index finger is perpetually extended straight as if pointing, the tendon severed by a swather's sickle blade.

"Do you like farming?" I ask, realizing I may have never asked this so directly. He started community college after high school, wanting to become a teacher, but during the fall harvest of his freshman year the family's hired man was killed when a grain partition collapsed and he was buried in corn. Dad returned home to help with the harvest that year and never left.

He nods and says, "Farming is fun until something goes wrong. When they call from the field because a combine is buried in mud, I have to stop everything to deal with the problem."

For the next several miles I quiz Dad about his grandparents, what he knows, what he remembers, why they became farmers. My great-grandparents' decision to farm led, in some way, to this morn-ing's drive: a farmer's daughter home from the city for a month, trying to preserve all that is changing, all that is no longer a part of my life but still lingers in my being, and Dad, a farmer's son, now a father of a farmer, driving the roads he has driven all of his life. Dad knows the basics about his grandparents' story, not much more.

"You should contact my cousin Pam, the one working on the family tree." He pauses and then adds, "Living each day is work enough for me without concerning myself with the past."

"I know, Dad," I laugh. My dad is a genius of the present moment, which is not helpful as I try to embrace my past. I am certain he could teach Eckhart Tolle a few things.

When I think about my dad—the first person I call when faced with life's practical challenges, like a broken car or a malfunctioning toilet, but the person to whom I avoid directly communicating anything personal, like being gay—I consider what we've held from each other over the years. It was on a drive like this one—just Dad and me—when he told me the truth about my grandmother's death. I was in my early twenties, and he and I were on our way home from a wedding. Dad was in the mood to talk, still buzzing from an evening with old cousins and family friends at the local fire hall. I was in the mood too, having spent the night studying distant relatives, trying to identify commonalities among all of us.

I had asked one simple question then: "Would you say you are more like your mother or father?" I'm sure I had asked Dad this before. His responses had been brief.

I knew the ways he was like my grandfather: he can have a short temper, is a hard worker, and is often charming and giving. But these characteristics account for only a small percentage of his composition. He is not tall and slender with brown eyes like my grandpa. Instead, he is shorter, stocky, with smoky blue eyes. I decided he must have been his mother's boy.

All of a sudden that night Dad took a deep breath and said, "Your grandmother killed herself. She was in a lot of pain. Nobody could figure out what was wrong with her."

The story of her death, one I had already pieced together from information passed through better-informed cousins, lingered in my mind as a child. Who was this woman? What was she like? What drove her to take her life by running a car in the garage? My curiosity about her was fueled by the fact that she lived on the farmstead where I was growing up. She had wandered the same roads, walked around the same farm, and yet she left the earth just months before I entered. Through my investigation I

learned that she had been sick, chronically ill, battling undiag-
nosed physical pain for years before she stopped the pain in a way
the doctors never could. She was loved, yet rarely mentioned at
holidays or barbecues. The story of her life was silenced that day,
along with her pain.

"I know," I responded as calmly as I could, as if I was trying
to pet the wings of a butterfly, not wanting it to fly away. Dad had
never spoken to me of the event, and I didn't want him to stop.

He went on to tell me much of what I already knew: she had
been sick for years; he had given her shots to stop the deep ach-
ing in her body, knowing that with every injection he was trading
the personality of the woman he loved for a drug-induced moment of painlessness.

That night on the long highway, my dad let go of a silence he
had held for years. Though he shared with me that night, we
haven't talked about it again. The butterfly is gone.

On our morning drive to the farm today our conversation didn't
go this deep, but Dad did oblige me by driving past his paternal
grandparents' first farmstead, which is about four miles from our
current farm. He also showed me a house in Barney where the
same grandparents retired after they left the farm. The house was
yellow, small, with a white shed and a clothesline. I looked out over
the field behind their house and wondered how many of their
stories had evaporated into the sky.

After about two hours of sorting, I take a break from my assignment and look down into the shop. A hired man is welding directly below me on ground level. To my right, through a large
garage door, I see the yard and a corner of the barn. To my left is
a larger room, an addition to the shop, which is as spacious as a
community center. The big doors—big enough to let a combine
drive in—are open, and I see, for the first time today, the land.

The fog has lifted and the land glistens like a fresh painting. This spacious view of the prairie is always shocking after being in the city. Though I've spent the largest percentage of my life in this landscape—in this openness—I always feel exposed. As a child when I visited my grandparents near the Bighorn Mountains in Wyoming I felt claustrophobic. The mountains seemed to block the sky and my eyes were forced to stop, when they were used to looking for miles across flat fields that didn't end, but simply rolled up into the sky. As an adult I've become accustomed to tight spaces, to being surrounded by buildings and people, to living in movement and chaos. In my current home I can't see past the houses that mirror mine on the other side of the street. So taking in the view of this flat expansive landscape is both startling and delightful. There is nowhere to hide. I am again part of the land.

I return to work, clamping and unscrewing parts. I pick up a cluster and at first think there are only two pieces to undo, but those two pieces break down into two more, and then into two more, like I am pulling apart wooden nesting dolls. When the cluster is disassembled I look for the pieces' home, reviewing my early-morning lesson of the cam locks, the barbed tees, and the closed nipples. I also make a pile of everything I can't categorize, along with things I am tripping over that must have a home somewhere in this shop.

Oddly, I am enjoying my work. I am focused. I am near my dad. The day is bright and crisp and I feel relaxed in a way I haven't in weeks.

When I come to a standstill, I ask Dad for a vacuum. Then I grab a mask and begin to suck up the sepia. With each motion of my arm, the sepia goes away, like I am scribbling on a kid's tablet where a white marker wets the page to reveal color.

In the afternoon I go down to the main floor to get my brother's help to finish a few of the pieces I couldn't get apart by myself. I drop my pile when a man walks into the shop.

Great, it's Randy. Randy is ten years older than me and was the absolute drop-dead hunk of all high school hunks when I was in elementary school. All of the girls were in love with him. Today he is a farmer, but I always thought he should turn in his tractor keys and make a fortune modeling.

"What, what is this!" Randy says, staring at me as if he's come upon a leprechaun. He lets out another burst: "Ha! What is this?" He is talking to someone just beyond my view, in the office, probably my dad. Again: "What is *this*?"

I am the "this" he is referring to. Me, standing by the vise, wrench in hand, covered in oil, dirt, and—likely—smelling of cat pee. I did not expect to encounter the public today. But I guess farmers must pop by each other's farms and socialize like office workers pop into cubicles.

After a short greeting and exchange, when I explain that I'm here to help over harvest, for the heck of it, I hear him say to the person beyond my sight, "And we complain about this place. Boy! I guess we must have it pretty good to have people coming back." I'm not sure if he's being sarcastic, but I pick up my next nipple and stay on task.

The Last Kiss

Jessica and I never talked about the *Friday Night Videos* night, never mentioned the absurd night of the kiss—how young and silly we were. So I started to believe that it didn't happen. After weeks, then months, then years of silence around the child's-play peck, my mind cast the entire episode as an illusion—no different than my daydreams—a reality only I knew. To this day I don't know if she would remember; we've never discussed it.

Four years later, Jessica still had not kissed a boy. The longer she abstained—looking for the perfect boy who was not to be found in Wyndmere—the more likely it was that I would escape the pain of having to hear about her *real* first kiss.

She talked about it, joked about it. "Melanie, I'll never kiss anyone."

"Yes, you will. You are just too picky. But really, I don't blame you." I tried to be supportive of her, because she would, at some point, probably kiss someone. Probably date someone. Probably have sex with someone. I had not yet had sex. When a few of my friends ventured into that world, I had decided to cling to my earlier convictions. I would not have sex until I was married. I figured I would probably get married, just like I had dated, gone to prom, and rolled around with horny young farmers. And I figured Jessica would too. And when we did, we would have each other, the relationship that really mattered.

During our high school years we spent our free time driving down gravel roads and talking. On Sunday afternoons, after leaving our Lutheran church, we headed into the heart of the country in her parents' car before settling into evenings of homework. I was always the passenger, with my feet on the dash and my hand holding my hair from my eyes as the wind swept through the open windows. Jessica was always the driver, singing at the top of her lungs. We were drawn to this routine by the rhythm of the gravel against the car, which was not too different from the meditative hush of a rainstorm.

My favorite roads were the primitive grass roads, which we didn't hesitate to take, even with her parents' Buick Park Avenue. The roads were bumpy, but not unmanageable. The grass brushing against the tires made it sound like we were in a car wash. Usually cottonwoods formed a canopy over the roads, a forest in the middle of the prairie. We often stopped to lie on the hood of the car and experience the wind and the quiet. I thought about confessing my feelings, which had deepened as the months and years passed. I had fallen in love, not just with her but with everything that was part of our time: the trees, the grass, the sky, the lightning storms, waiting for each other in the halls of the school, late nights, movies, talks, music.

I didn't know how it would work out exactly. I knew our relationship was not typical. I knew Jessica was not like the other people in my life. I knew that I too was different, with my secret love no one else seemed to have. Not even Jessica, who knew almost everything there was to know, seemed to understand. At least she never said anything. In North Dakota the idea of two girls together didn't come up—ever. The idea was as foreign as living in a city, with thousands of people breathing the same air. The people of the prairie gave me no context for my feelings. And yet the entire idea of being with a woman, being in love with a woman, was so deeply ingrained in my being I couldn't dismiss it, not even as my physical reality begged me to reconsider the sanity of it all.

This was at the cusp of our now recent history, the time before gay and lesbian people routinely showed up on TV. This was before people were fighting in the mainstream about gay rights or gay marriage. This was the time before Ellen came out and before Clay Aiken was a blip on the radar. This was before *Will & Grace* even. The fact that we didn't get cable on the farm meant that in all of my nineteen years in North Dakota, I saw two references to lesbians on TV. One was a made-for-TV movie about two suburban moms falling in love. I pretended to vacuum my parents' bedroom that evening while everyone in my family was downstairs, so I could watch without getting caught. The other was a talk show where the host interviewed a very feminine woman and an extremely masculine woman, trying to identify who was a truer lesbian. Besides these minor glances, I did not have any experiences to contradict what I knew about marriage, men and women, or the ways of North Dakota, where there was a particular formula for what was considered normal or abnormal. For the most part, this formula was simple: anything not visible in North Dakota is probably abnormal.

Jessica, in her wisdom, never said, "You know, I think there is something between us," as she might have. She very well could have approached it intellectually, as she did most things, saying, "I have researched the root of women's friendships. There is a long history of romantic friendship, especially in the nineteenth century. I think we happen to be in one of those relationships, which is expected to last between ten and twelve years, given that we are best friends and all." This would have been her approach, I think now.

We heard a couple of stories about boys who had called us "lesbos" behind our back. I froze when I heard this. The air seemed thin, like I was going to faint, like someone had opened a door into my mind. I also knew, however, that in all likelihood they were not talking about me but about Jessica. She was the one, after all, who was uninhibited when grabbing my arm or showing affection; she was the one who had not kissed boys. Still, their joke, which I doubt they even believed, stuck a pin into a deep secret I had not revealed. And they named something I had not named. Jessica, however, didn't flinch when she heard the rumors. She only rolled her eyes, not the least bit worried, concerned, or interested. I studied her, to see if she too was hiding a secret. As far as I could tell, there was nothing: no shame, no worry, no hidden emotions. And yet there was something between us that even some stupid boys were able to see. Or was there?

My life wasn't entirely built around Jessica. I had other friends both in my grade and hers. And while Jessica preferred to go to movies or stay home on the weekends, I sometimes chose to be with the rest of my friends who were doing what high school kids on the edge of North Dakota do. On Friday nights, we hung outside Cenex waiting for the gang to gather. When everyone was accounted for we piled into the backs of pickups and drove into the dark country where we made big fires and wrapped ourselves in blankets. After a while the boys got drunk and started running through the fire to show that they wouldn't get burned. Next, couples disappeared into the woods. I watched all of this, wanting to be connected, not wanting to be left out. On many of these nights, when everyone else went off with their girlfriends and boyfriends, I went to Jessica's house. We drank root beer—she refused to dabble in alcohol—watched movies, and talked into the night.

Years after the *Friday Night Videos* night, Jessica wanted to practice kissing. She was a junior, I was a sophomore. She turned to me before we fell asleep one night when I was staying at her house and said, without fear, "I think we should practice."

"Practice what?" I asked, having no idea what she was talking about. She could have wanted to get up and practice her trumpet or go to the shop and shoot hoops. That was Jessica, always wanting to improve, always practicing.

"Getting ourselves ready." She turned to me in bed. Her face was purple in the light cast from the farmyard.

"Yes. Ready for what?" I repeated. "Look, I am not going to get up and exercise right now."

She kept talking, not acknowledging the sarcasm in my voice. "I think the next time we are at a party with Todd and Brad—"

She stopped, reconsidering her approach. "Well, here." In that moment she grabbed my hand from under the covers where it was tucked by my side and pulled it into the air. She wasn't going to explain her actions; she was just going to show me what she wanted. "First, let's pretend that I am Todd."

Todd, at the time, was my semi-boyfriend. We had been good friends since we were in fifth grade. People always tried to pair us up, like loose socks that needed to be tucked together. In tenth grade, he had a renewed interest in me. We flirted and talked on the phone and, at the last several parties, he had wanted to make out. I couldn't do it. I lied, telling him he was so special that I wanted to wait for the right moment. This was odd since we weren't even talking about sex. We were talking about a simple kiss and I couldn't bring myself to do it. Surprisingly he settled for my explanation along with some long hugs when I allowed him to rub his lips against my cheek.

Jessica and I laughed about this, how ironic it was that I could make out with the other boys but just could not bring myself to kiss Todd. Something about him was too brotherly. But he was also a good and reliable topic of discussion and deliberation between us.

Brad was Jessica's Todd. He had been obsessed with her since junior high. Because I knew Jessica, I wasn't too worried about Brad, though—out of all of the guys in Wyndmere—he was the one that she might have considered. He, like Jessica, seemed slightly out of place, but only because of his oddly un-farm-like fashion sense. On basketball game days when the boys on the team had to dress up, he wore expensive clothes—like Calvin Klein— while the rest of the boys were dressed in sweaters their moms had bought at Herberger's. He was also a good athlete, with a polished body and a chiseled face, so Jessica wasn't overly horrified to have his attention. Holding hands with Brad at a ninth-grade party was the only contact she had ever had with a boy.

I teased her about Brad and I obsessed about my situation with Todd. This was how it was supposed to be. They were almost imaginary figures because so much of our time was spent discussing them but not actually seeing them.

In the purple light, Jessica put her head back down on the pillow and scooted close to me. We were holding hands and my heart was racing. "All right, we're holding hands," she said, starting a play-by-play. "And I'm getting closer. Hmm. Let's see. And I start to run my hand up your arm."

"Turn to me." I turned to face her. "Okay. Remember, I'm Todd."

I realized at that point that I should play along, should play the role I had established with Todd to make this all seem valid. "Well, I don't *want* to kiss him. I can't even imagine it," I said, though in that moment it suddenly seemed impossible that she and I had stayed at each other's houses, year after year, and our lips had not touched once.

"We have to try," she said, inching her face closer. "He's coming closer to you. You can feel his breath on your nose." Still holding my hand, she propped herself on her elbow and rested a few inches from my face.

"Now, just imagine that I *am* him and you *want* to kiss me." She leaned down and kissed my lips softly. I didn't react at first, scared to reveal anything. I rolled toward her, more relaxed. Her breath had the faintest scent of corn. After a brief moment, she backed away.

"There. Easy," she said, like a teacher coaching me through a math problem. It felt backward that she was teaching me how to kiss. However, this was our dynamic. She was always my teacher, always the one who put me on course. Even when I was the expert we switched roles so that she could assume the role she knew best—the leader in everything.

I fell to my back. My chest filled with the feeling of a fluid love, a sensation I had chased in my imagination since I had been four years old. I was, for the brief moment, completely satisfied, without another need in the world. I wonder if that feeling—the pure glistening feeling that makes everything brilliant—is the sole reason people pursue love. I will feel this same emotion only a handful of times in my life.

"Your turn," she said.

"My turn?" I asked, not wanting to make any move to indicate that we were doing something she should feel strange about. As long as boys were a part of it, it seemed fine.

"Yes. I want to imagine that Brad is behind me. Like at the New Year's Eve party. When we were all on the floor."

Weeks earlier Jessica had started to talk about this whole kissing thing after she had agreed to go to a New Year's Eve party. Because I knew Brad was going to be there, that we would all pair up, I started to ask her if she would finally break her kissing ban. I wanted to be prepared.

"Are you going to kiss Brad?"

"I doubt it. His lips might be chapped." Jessica looked at me from where she sat on my bed. I had negotiated with my parents to turn the downstairs office into my bedroom. The carpet was gray-and-black shag. I had lined my shelves with pictures of my friends and high school symbols of achievement—ribbons, medals, dried flowers from homecoming and proms.

"Are you going to kiss Todd?"

"I don't know. It still freaks me out."

"They are going to want to kiss us. Maybe that's all they want." Jessica said, lying on my bed. "I don't even understand the purpose of these parties. Make-out parties. That's all they are. Do *not* leave me. Stay close all night. I just don't know if I am ready."

At the party the four of us had sat in a row at the foot of a couch. When the lights dimmed and everyone sunk under covers, the four of us slid down to the floor like siblings sharing a bed. Brad and Todd curled behind us in spooning positions. Jessica and I turned to each other. In the dark she whispered to me, "I am not doing it."

"Me neither," I whispered back. For the next couple of hours we stayed close, giggling and talking, while the boys punched each other over us and we all watched a movie.

So when she said, "Like at the party," I knew exactly what she wanted. When she turned away from me, I shifted behind her body, followed the curves and bends in her posture so that we were perfect matches. Because I was still hesitant, she had to reach back and pull my arm over her side.

"Yes. Exactly like this," she said, satisfied with my grasp around her side. "Now, I am going to turn and you pretend to be him, coming behind me, trying to kiss me."

"Okay," I whispered. I waited a few seconds and released her hand. Then, gently, I moved my face to the back of her neck.

"Kiss my neck," she suggested.

"Okay," I said again and kissed her on her neck. She didn't have to instruct me any further. It felt natural for me to repeat this, kissing her gently, remembering years ago when she had started at my neck and moved up to my mouth. I slowly worked from her neck to her cheek to her lips, which met me as she twisted her body. After I was done—not wanting to extend my kissing past what would have been normal for our experiment—I sank down next to her.

When we finally fell asleep, I felt full, fed, but now also I knew the pain that comes with love, a desperate need, a craving that could push you to give up everything. I felt like Violet Beauregarde in *Charlie and the Chocolate Factory*, who could not resist the three-course-meal gum, even if it meant giving up a chance for so much more. Before that night I had simply fed my need for love with daydreams. Now everything seemed more complicated. This reality struck me the next day when we went to church and Jessica acted like nothing had happened. She did not hold my gaze for an extra second. Did not touch my hand. Did not invite me over for the night. My desperation was not so much about wanting to kiss her again. It was that now, more than ever, I could not imagine losing her. Her graduation was one year away.

That night I cried. The cry was so deep my organs seemed to leave my body through my running nose. But I did not make a sound. Instead, in the silence of the night, I swallowed my sadness, wiped my eyes, and went to sleep.

Yoga in the Air

Harvest retreat, day two. I am fired. Twice. My morning does not move quickly. I am on vacation, after all—and I just can't heed the 6:00 a.m. alarm clock. On my drive to the farm (I missed the commute with Dad), I stop in Barney, where my brother David just started a new job selling seed to farmers. His job in online sales at a family-owned retail business was looking bleak due to the economy, and my uncle needed help with the family seed business. Even though he has to drive an hour each morning from Fergus Falls, Dave decided to quit his job and give seeds a try.

The building Dave works in used to be Barney Bean Plant, located just off the highway and across from a graveyard at the edge of town. When I get out of my car I leap over big puddles of standing water to get to the door. I've never been in the building, so I walk through a couple of doors until I find my brother in a bright but outdated, carpeted office. Posters picturing dark green shoots and leaves bursting through the ground decorate the walls. Dave gives me a tour of the large, echoing, mostly empty building.

Dave and his coworker Bill are getting ready to pull a big wagon-like thing called a weigh cart into the field. Apparently the business provides a grain-weighing service to customers. The weigh cart helps farmers calibrate the yield monitor on their combines, compare the yields of different varieties of crops, or get early yield readings. After Dave explains all of this, he asks me if I want to ride along.

"I don't know. I *am* late for my unofficial start time on the farm," I say, holding back a yawn. What I don't say is that the weigh cart work sounds sort of boring.

"Oh, come on. You want to know all about farming, don't you?" Dave says. "That's why you're home."

"What if Dad's expecting me?" I ask.

"You're already fired because you didn't show up this morning. I talked to Donny," Dave says.

I figured as much. "All right, guess I'll come," I say, knowing my dad isn't holding his breath for my arrival.

We jump in the pickup and take off. After about eight miles we turn down a dirt road covered by a canopy of tree limbs. Ahead I see deep, muddy ruts and wonder if we'll get stuck with this crazy wagon behind us. I realize I should know better when Bill hits the four-wheel drive and we plow through the mud. Up on our left is a field, which we identify as our destination because it is the only place with machinery. The field is fully harvested, aside from two strips of crop that will be harvested for the weighing experiment.

I get out and wander around while Bill and Dave get set up. All I can think about, standing in this field, is how strangely odd and wonderful this moment is. Here I am, standing on the earth. How often do I actually walk on the bare, cement-free earth? Due to the recent wet days, the ground is moist and gives under my feet. Each step is like bouncing on an angel food cake.

Dave comes over to me, plucks a brown, dry pod from a two-foot-high stalk, and opens it. I study the pod and its white balls.

"Those soy beans?" I say, wanting validation of my knowledge.

"Yup. This is what your fake meat is made of." He pops some balls into his mouth and hands me one.

"I can eat this?"

"Uh-huh," he says, awaiting my reaction.

I roll the little ball around in my mouth and bite down. The middle is gummy and the overwhelming flavor is not actually a flavor but a burst of earth, of freshness. "Not bad." I pick another dried pod from a stalk and toss a few more balls into my mouth. They don't taste anything like a meatless chicken patty, but they will do.

We walk back to the weigh cart where a farmer stands with his arms crossed and watches his hired man suck up soybeans with the combine. The combine is like a moving building. I am shorter than its tires. I proudly note that they are using a John Deere combine, an important detail. In these parts your farm machinery is either John Deere (green) or International (red), and brand loyalty runs a hundred years deep. Since we are a John Deere family, I figure the farmer is probably on my dad's good side.

When the hired man turns from the last row and drives toward us, I feel the same rush in my body as I do when the jets of an airplane fire up and lift me into the air. I am in awe of innovation.

I walk up to the farmer. *Hmm. What to say?* "You must be the owner of this, um, field, eh?" I ask. He is wearing a black T-shirt, cap, jeans, and leather work boots. I'm unsure of his age. Lines in his face indicate experience, but his hair is still very black.

"Yup. I guess I must be," he says, smiling. After a bit of chit-chat, when I learn that he farms with his brother and his son—who recently came back to farm—he tells me that he retired ten years ago.

I look at him with a questioning scowl and scan the field around us. "So, is this what a retired farmer looks like?" I holler over the noise of the combine emptying the soybeans into the weigh cart in front of us.

"I guess it must be. Yup. I'd go crazy without something to do," he shouts back.

The farmer version of retirement is certainly not retirement in the way I envision it for myself, where I line up books, movies, recipes, projects, and trips. When not reading, I'd loll around like a cat in patches of sun. After a long, self-indulgent, gluttonous break from work, I'd figure out what bigger purpose I could contribute my efforts toward.

Retirement is more of a label on the farm than a full-fledged reality. It indicates graduation of sorts into a slower pace. Instead of getting up at 5:00 a.m., retired farmers can get up at 6:30 a.m. Instead of working all winter, they can take a few more weeks off and turn the mundane labor over to the next generation or the hired help.

After a lifetime of working this land, it is probably impossible for farmers to sit home on a day when the leaves are golden, the sky is indigo, the air is still warm, and the rest of the rural world is going about the business of harvest. The same retirement pattern happened with my grandpa and I suspect it will happen with my dad too. They don't stay away; they keep coming back, like migratory monarchs return north. And maybe farmers' inability to truly retire makes sense to me. After all, here I am—after years of being away—standing in a field, talking with a farmer, and watching soybeans fall like hail into a cart.

My presence is probably a bit odd. There are four men in this field. I am the only woman, wearing a new green Pioneer seed baseball cap I got from Dave this morning, lipstick, ripped jeans, and tennis shoes. The hat looks good, I think. I pretend to belong while they all look at the scale, write a few calculations on paper, punch numbers into a calculator, figure out how much crop they just harvested, ask the farmer about the moisture content of the crop, remind each other how many feet are in a rod (which I look up later: 16.5), and then calculate a final number.

"Guess you won't have to apply for food stamps this year," Bill says to the farmer. Perhaps I am reading too much into it, but on the farmer's face I see something anticipatory, like you'd see in a man waiting to hear his name called at a raffle. These numbers tell him what his yield will be, how the crop is looking. These numbers are utterly confusing to me, but for him they are the answer to a season of work.

"That's good. Not sure where I'd go for that," the farmer responds. And I gather, from the jovial nature of the small group, that these numbers are good news; the bean harvest is going well.

When we return to Barney, Dave and I decide to have lunch at the bar in town, DJ's. Since I've already been fired, there's no need to rush to the farm. Plus I'm excited to experience my first restaurant meal back in the middle of nowhere.

Inside DJ's I scan the space. There are three booths, a bar, a pool table, posters with race-car drivers, and random stuff sitting in the windowsill, like a double-sided puzzle with Dalmatians, "the world's hardest jigsaw," or so the box claims. Six other people are in the bar, including our waitress and the cook.

Dave and I sit down and browse the menu. I am in what is considered the breadbasket of the country and I can't order anything natural, at least what "natural" means in my world—leafy greens, tempeh sandwich, fresh squash soup. I order a cheese pizza and a Corona (beer at lunch is rare for me, but I'm rewarding myself for a day and a half well done). Not wanting to offend rural custom, I am too self-conscious to request a lime when the Corona comes naked.

My brother orders cheese balls and the special: chicken, boiled potatoes, canned green beans, and fruit cocktail. The cheese balls, which I haven't had in at least fifteen years, are heavenly.

Over lunch, Dave and I catch up on life. As he talks I study his eyes. They are dark blue, the color of ink. They are same eyes that looked at me from behind the bars of his crib after he was born. I've always thought of myself as so much older than him, but we are only twenty-one months apart. For the first years of my life, Dave was my best friend. Mom used to pull us in a wagon down the dirt road in front of our little green house. The wheels of our red wagon were squeaky. As they turned, they crushed clumps of dried mud like a baker might crush walnuts with a rolling pin. Mom lined the wagon with colorful woven rugs from the kitchen to absorb the shock of the hard earth. On those trips I was in charge of holding my baby brother as he sat, tucked tightly between my legs, in the nest sculpted by Mom.

How time flies, I think, as we take the last few bites of our gut-wrenching meal, swear off heavy food, and get up to leave.

In my food-induced coma I almost don't hear a man sitting at the end of the bar when he says, "You should tell your dad to buy you a new pair of pants."

I look down, startled, and realize that my shredded retro Levi's probably do look a little beat up if you don't realize I'm working. Don't realize I am a farmer.

"You're right," I say, "he should!"

"Cheap bastard," the man says, looking up at the TV, shaking his head, and taking another drag on his cigarette. I don't know him but I am pretty sure he must know my dad and, by extension, me.

"Well, you be sure to deliver that message next time you see him," I say, stepping out of the door.

"Oh, I will," he says.

I am certain there will be a conversation one of these harvest nights, when Dad stops in for a beer, about a daughter who came back from the city and—poor thing, doesn't he see—needs a decent pair of pants.

After my morning with David I finally make my way to the farm. I tell Dad I wasn't sloughing off. Rather, I was helping out with the other side of the family business. He looks at me suspiciously and tells me I can help him finish building steps. The steps will lead up to a small plateau where trucks drive up and dump grain into holding tanks in the ground. The grain is sucked from the holding tanks into bins, then into a dryer, then into cooling bins, then up a grain leg, and finally to storage bins where it will sit until sold.

Now, if I needed steps I would buy them or hire someone to build them. But here, on the farm, Dad creates everything he needs. He has already cut most of the wood and has driven stakes into the ground to hold the frame. He places planks on the frame and shows me where to drill holes and then insert screws. I go about the project as he has shown me, until a pile of boards turns into a new set of steps.

When I am done, a couple of hours later, I feel a sense of accomplishment with a tangible product in front of me. And my mind is completely empty. Words and problems and buzz of conference calls are not lingering in my body.

My second firing of the day happens after I go to visit with a cousin of mine who pulls into the yard to say hello. After catching up and sharing with her that I'm home for a month to work as a farmer, I return to find my brother who, after he fires me, tells me that my final task for the day is to climb to the top of the grain leg with him to oil some bearings.

The leg is the skyscraper of the farm. It reaches beyond the top of the barn, beyond the top of the tallest trees. The structure is little more than a metal ladder running next to something that looks like a furnace vent, with platforms at three different levels. I stare at the leg leading up into the sky, and remember how as a foolish teenager I climbed the grain elevator in Wyndmere in the middle of the night. One wrong step, one missed rung, and you fall from the sky to your end.

"I'm not going up there. No way in hell. " I look at my brother like he's crazy.

"Come on, Mel."

"I could die."

"You will not die."

"Do you get scared?"

"No. The view's incredible," he says in a slightly singsong voice.

I think about this for a second. "Really? What's it like?"

"Oh. You can see for miles," he smirks, knowing he's making progress. "I'll go behind you. If you fall you'll just fall into me." I look up into the sky and consider the option of using my brother as a safety net.

"What if I fall where the cage things aren't around us?" I say. Outside of the rungs are cages that would at least help you from falling out and away from the leg, but wouldn't stop you from falling straight down to your death.

"You won't. Come on! You have to. This is part of the experience." Donny is challenging me, just like David challenged me that morning. Not fair.

In my opinion Donny shouldn't be climbing to the top of this thing either. The entire set-up looks horribly primitive in the sense that there is not an elevator to safely take us to the top. But I can't resist the view, and the dare, so I grab the first rung and start my climb.

I have not bungee-jumped, have not parachuted out of an airplane, have not flown down a zip line. These are activities I don't particularly care if I don't do in my life. But here I am instead, climbing to the top of a leg. At least with daredevil sports you have professional supervision. You get to wear safety belts or have another human strapped to you as insurance. But here it is just my brother and me, with no safety nets, no insurance, no protection. With every step my stomach flips, my arms feel shaky.

"Sure you don't want to grab onto this part? Might be easier." I look down between my legs and see my brother tapping on the rung. I am not holding onto the rungs, but to the outside of the handrails, wrapping my forearms around the ladder, doing more of a shimmy than a climb.

"No!" I scream.

When we get to the first level I scoot my butt over onto the platform and look up. There are two more levels. "I'm not going any farther, this is just fine," I say. "Pretty view," I add, to tell him I'm content.

"You've come this far and you won't go to the top?" he shouts at me. He has to shout because it is windy and everything is rattling like we are in a hurricane. I am scared and have almost lost my hat several times on the way up.

"Ughh. All right," I say and continue to work my way up. My shaking gets worse with each step.

At the second platform the wind is even stronger. My brother has to climb in front of me because the wind makes the door too heavy for me to lift. He holds the door and I scurry onto the next platform. "I can't go on," I say.

My brother shakes his head and points to the top, which is about ten feet away. "Are you sure you really want to stop here when you are so close? You'll actually feel safer on the top, there is a railing all the way around."

"Fine!" I yell.

We climb the last ten rungs to final platform. On the top I crawl while Donny stands up and walks to the other side. He lies down and reaches to oil the bearing below the platform. The entire leg is swaying in the wind.

"I guess it is sort of a windy day," my brother yells at me, grinning, without an ounce of fear in his being.

"Is this wind normal?" I ask.

"Nah, not really. It's pretty windy," he says and chuckles.

The wind in North Dakota is said to have driven some of the early settlers to insanity. Therefore, "pretty windy" can be equated to a mini-hurricane, quite capable (I believe in this moment) of lifting me from the platform.

When I finally get the courage to pull myself to a standing position and look out, seventy-five feet above the ground, conquering my terror turns out to be a worthy investment. Farmland is made for this, a view from the sky. I see for miles and the openness washes over me, into me. From here the farm is one holistic entity. And the colors of the earth are those of harvest: gold crops, black earth, white grasses, yellow roads, all contrasted by the blue sky. I think back to the day I wrote my mantra, when I was looking out of my window at a church steeple, dreading a day of conference calls and stabbing pain. And here I am now: I can spread my arms, stretch my body to the sky in a sort of advanced yoga pose that carries me into infinity. This freedom is what I've been craving. And perhaps I have just learned—in a palpable way—that freedom can never be the fruit of routine, only of risk.

On our way down my fear subsides with each step. I am no longer anticipating what might happen. I am no longer resisting. Instead I breathe with each new rung (which I am now using), glad that I am here, hanging above the farm, crazy as it is. I am— at least for now, at least for the next month—free.

Born Again for the First Time

Shortly after Jessica and I became friends, God rode into Wyndmere on the shoulders of the new girl's B-squad basketball coach, a man who had the presence of an ancient Egyptian pharaoh. Coach was tall, handsome, muscular, and bow-legged. His shoulders were broad, his jaw was strong, and each of his flexed calves had a ledge. He wore expensive pressed shirts with colorful, crisp ties, fitted pants, and shiny shoes. He was out of place in the world of farmers, whose bodies were bulky, meaty, and strong, not sculpted and packaged into neat pastel suits.

Coach was not Lutheran, Catholic, or Methodist—the three choices we had available. He was a born-again Christian and went to a church in Wahpeton. This, at the time in our small town, was abnormal.

Jessica was the best player on our basketball team. Coach immediately identified her as his protégée. After we finished our regular practice he'd often make her stay behind and work an extra half an hour, knowing that she was our only hope of success as a team. "What are you *doing?*" his booming voice would echo in the gym. I often watched, doing my homework on the sideline while I waited for Jessica to be free. "You need to keep your wrist straight! Come on. *Think*, kid. You are *better* than this!"

Jessica immediately took to Coach like she took to all of her newfound passions. As he pushed her, she pushed herself further. This pushing involved joining him and some of the boys after school and on the weekends for weight training. Coach was convinced weights would improve her shot.

Shortly into the weight-lifting sessions, Coach started to introduce God to Jessica's training routine. "You need to turn to the
Lord, *little girl*," he'd say, sounding like God himself, walking a
circle around her, with his arms crossed and a whistle hanging
around his neck. Jessica just concentrated, her eyes glistening
with emotion, pushing herself. Then he'd back off, start to walk
nonchalantly beside her. "God has everything you need. The
strength. The perfection. The will. You've just got to surrender,
kid." At that point he'd shrug his shoulders, as if to say that this
was the easiest thing in the world, if she could only grasp what he
was telling her. I'd catch glimpses of him grooming her and then
hear the rest from Jessica.

I had not heard anyone talk about God the way Coach
talked to Jessica. Growing up in North Dakota, God wasn't a
question, as in "Do you believe?" God just was. God was in
charge of everything, and so we prayed for health, for the crops,
and for our football team to win on Friday nights. Nobody in
high school spoke about God, though we all went about our
church duties like confirmation, first communion, Bible school,
and church on Sundays.

I believed, as Mom taught me, that I was not alone. God was
always near. And I believed God was as real and mysterious as fire,
air, or light. Each of these elements, like God, was impossible to
hold, but necessary and undeniably real. The God I felt in the
wind and in the grass was close, personal, the only entity that
knew everything about me from the time I was little to the time I
started grappling with my secret feelings for Jessica.

In the early years I spent Sunday mornings at Antelope Methodist, a country church near a creek and surrounded by fields.
Antelope had a fragile balcony and creaky pine floors. I went to
Bible school for one week every summer. This is where I first met
the church version of Jesus, although at the time I thought Jesus
was Elvis. On those mornings I tore Elvis—dressed in his holy
white robes—from our workbooks, and glued his head to Popsicle

sticks for our puppet shows. These projects left my fingers covered in glue balls that reminded me of my own skin.

After church on Sunday mornings I ate cookies and listened to the stories of farmers. These men and women were generous people who often braved the gravel roads to pull a traveling stranger out of a ditch, even on blizzard days when the temperatures plummeted to fifty degrees below zero. In keeping with my experiences later on, I rarely heard the farmers mention God outside of church; instead they demonstrated their faith through devotion to neighbor and stranger alike.

Within a few weeks of Coach's counseling—both spiritual and athletic—Jessica frequently talked about God, even outside of church. She started closing her notes to me with "In Him, Jessica." The "Him" she was referring to was, of course, Jesus Christ. After her closing she also included a Bible verse. I held these notes until I got home, anxious to look up the verses as if they were secret codes, riddled with hidden meaning. Often, the words in the Bible passages were full of love. This was a deeper love, a new love, something we were now uncovering together. And soon I too hunted for Bible passages to include at the end of my notes to her, to convey my commitment to her and to God.

Soon after the Bible verses, we started listening to Christian music. The music had a powerful effect on both of us. Enchanting voices and beautiful instruments carried the impassioned stories about lives being turned around after seeing *the light*. When we stayed at each other's houses we set our stereo alarms to play our favorite songs from Steven Curtis Chapman, Twila Paris, or the Newsboys. When the world was still hazy with twilight, fresh with a new beginning, the music filled the room, gradually getting louder, and roused us from bed. Barely awake, I had the sensation of being coated with warm honey. I had Jessica. I had God. And I now had salvation.

As soon as this new world opened up to us we saw, immediately and clearly, that everyone around us didn't get it. They had blinders on. They were still living in a world of gray, void of color. If they too could gain this understanding of how God could save them, they would be free! If they could repent from their sinful existences, they would be reborn into salvation! Our job was to rescue and love these lost sheep, our parents, our friends, our classmates. Our job was to help them understand the vast, amazing world that would open up to them once God rescued them from their miseries. We scoured the pews of regulars at the Lutheran church, shaking our heads at their misled, stagnant repetition of rhyme and verse. They were missing the spirit we heard in the stories of the Christian music; stories from voices who sang about how their lives were changed by God, how their lives were lived for God, how they were put on the earth to witness, to transform, to share the incredible truth of the Lord!

We started wearing Christian T-shirts to school to help bear witness to our lost peers. Each day we also pinned a tiny silver cross on the collar of our shirts. The cross, about the size of a pinky tip, was not just a sign of my commitment to the Lord—it was also the symbol that connected me to Jessica. I knew that regardless of where I was, Jessica would be wearing our tiny matching cross.

From the outside, my new relationship with God was the most conspicuous form of acting out I did as a teenager. My love and commitment to God was more transparent than my love for Jessica. My parents, probably uncomfortable with my new, zealous expressions, didn't really say anything.

The only insight I had about my parents' thoughts came from Dad one night on our way to a basketball tournament. "I heard that the new church in Wahpeton is some sort of joint where they stand during the sermon. Wave their arms. Sing hallelujah or something," he said.

"Yeah?" I asked, in a confrontational tone that clearly came off as "Yeah, and what about it?"

"Yeah?" He mimicked my tone as he did when he thought I was acting too big for my britches, as he put it.

"Well. I think it is a little over the top. All that rolling of eyes, singing hallelujah." He looked out over the crops, as he always did when we were in the car. "All that holier than thou talk."

Dad never talked about God, really, though he went to church regularly and ushered most Sundays. I watched him drop money into the felt-lined wooden offering dish, which seemed to me like a great act of faithfulness, as I wasn't sure what the money bought us exactly. But I had now determined that our regular routine and commitment wasn't enough. The Lutheran church was too quiet, too humble, too off-key. At the Lutheran church we didn't express any emotion or true and heartfelt devotion to God. And so I knew Dad couldn't understand.

"Well, *personally*, I think actually praising God makes a lot more sense than what we do every Sunday," I said, lit with anger. "All we ever do is repeat the same phrases from that green book over and over and over. Nobody cares. Nobody means what they say." I felt like a witness. I was being challenged and it was my duty to stand up for the Lord, though I stopped short of implicating myself. "At least *those* people care about God."

Coach told Jessica about youth gatherings in other towns, retreats where we could meet and share "community" with other young believers. Wanting to know what it would be like to meet other people who understood our deep commitment to God, we signed up for retreat in Valley City one weekend.

Everything was different at the rally, a new world. A rock band played Christian music. People whispered under their breath "Praise Jesus" while listening to speakers. Kids wore crosses and Christian T-shirts, just like us. We broke out into small groups to talk about what it meant to be a witness.

At the retreat I heard people talk about "homosexuality" for the first time in my life. I was sitting in a circle with my small group. Jessica was in another. Halfway through a session where we were learning how to bring messages from the retreat back to the real world, a small pimply-faced boy raised his hand and asked what God thought about homosexuality.

"Ah, yes, homosexuality. Quite the subject," said the adult leader. I suddenly began to feel uneasy as he talked about the sin, one of the worst. This thing, this *word* even, was unnatural, representing a death, in fact, of something natural.

I didn't identify with the word *homosexual*. Sex didn't seem to be my issue—I was full of emotion, not lust. Still, I was uneasy and curious. And while they talked, I dismissed the connection as best I could, figuring that the adults at the retreat couldn't know the full answer because they didn't know what they were talking about. Jessica, our friendship, our love, our devotion to God, was the purest form of love in the world. My love for her couldn't be a sin. In fact, my love was the opposite of a sin because I lived my love for her as a witness to the Lord. There had to be another word. There had to be another expression. There had to be another way to talk about loving someone more than one would love a husband.

Small-Town Tour

A few days after climbing the leg I am in the filthy car—there is no way to keep it clean around here—and turning into Cayuga as part of my small-town tour. Today's road trip, a self-orchestrated 145-mile loop around the rural world, will take me to several small towns in North Dakota near where I grew up. Most of these towns I haven't been to in twenty years, and some of the towns I've never seen. Today I've already toured Mantador, population 71; Hankinson, population 1,058; Lidgerwood, population 738; Geneseo, population unknown (at least I couldn't find it online). I have Cayuga, population 61, and Rutland, population 220, yet to explore.

I'm not sure what it is about finding life and activity in the middle of nowhere that causes a sweet rise in my chest. Perhaps my excitement comes from growing up with the story of Hansel and Gretel or maybe my passion is just a by-product of growing up in a place without a lot of people, always wanting to discover activity. Today, from afar, over a grove of trees, I'll see a silhouette of a grain elevator, church steeple, or a water tower, and feel like I've discovered penicillin—ridiculous but true.

In 2008 the world's urban population total finally started to exceed that of the world's rural population. In the past fifty years nearly two-thirds of rural counties in the Great Plains lost at least one-third of their population. In North Dakota, forty-seven of the state's fifty-three counties lost population between 2000 and 2005.

I remember being in a Minneapolis coffee shop a few years ago when I saw that North Dakota senator Byron Dorgan, along with a Nebraska senator, had introduced in Congress what they called the New Homestead Act. Dorgan described this act as "a tool for rural areas seeking to halt chronic out-migration, or population loss, and economically revitalize rural communities." Not knowing the details, I immediately imagined Melissa and me claiming some land, begging our loved ones to follow us to little farmsteads on the plains. In our barn we'd set up—I don't know— a music studio, a writing loft, an easel, a pottery corner, and a room for traveling artists to stay as they passed through. The proposed legislation was never passed into law.

I wonder if halting the loss is possible. This morning I've stopped to study the remnants of what look like old grocery stores, general stores, community centers, and houses. The paint on these buildings is peeling, walls and roofs are sinking, but worn lettering indicates that at one time these structures were essential, cared for, and whole—that they belonged to someone. There are few humans visible in the smallest of these towns, aside from those I see in the distance stepping out of their homes to grab the mail or to beat a rug.

In Lidgerwood and Hankinson I have talked with the pharmacy and hardware store owners who happen to also be my sister-in-law's siblings. They are my age and running businesses in the towns, which astounds me. The townspeople are supportive and want them to succeed, I learned. The streets were bustling, reminding me of my earliest memories of Wyndmere.

But the still smaller towns, like Cayuga, where I sit now, and Mantador and Geneseo, towns I explored earlier, are tragically beautiful in the way only places that hold the enchantment of abandonment can be. The buildings are empty, collapsing slowly. The towns are like crawfish that have died, leaving their beautiful exoskeletons behind.

A few days after this drive I'm paging through a history book and find a 1909 postcard with a bird's-eye view of Cayuga. The

caption below the postcard says the town had a population of
1,564 and—at the time—a hotel, hardware store, flour mill, newspaper, creamery, garage, livery stable, merchandisers, saloons, and
a depot. Today in Cayuga the only gathering places I can discern
are a run-down bar and a church, places that help people escape
their lives. There is metaphor in what remains, I think.

My hometown has changed significantly over the last hundred
years. Wyndmere began with the merger of two villages, Moselle
and East Wyndmere, in 1889, at the place where the Soo Line
(Minneapolis, St. Paul, and Sault Ste. Marie) and Northern Pa-
cific (NP) Railroads crossed. The NP put up the first four buildings
in town: depot, section house, water tank, and loading dock. Soon
a general store, hardware store, two elevators, real estate offices,
and houses emerged on the small piece of land. Other businesses
came and went in the early years: barber shops, a creamery, a
livery barn, gas stations, cafés, hotels, farm implement dealers, a
newspaper, banks, sellers of motor vehicles, and even—doing
business in 1954—Vertin's Furniture and Funeral Home. The
town supported whatever was needed, whatever made sense for
the people, even a business that both provided for life's comforts
and comforted after life slipped away.

In my earliest memory of Wyndmere, I am standing in Johnson's Store. Johnson's was on the main street, kitty-corner from
the bus barn, across the street from the creamery, near the lumberyard, next to the grocery store, and just down the block from
the café. Mr. Johnson, the fourth generation of his family to run
the store in its seventy-four-year history, had a squat, oval face and
red cheeks. His hands were set like large lobster claws—as if there
was only one joint between his thumb and the rest of his fingers—
well suited to scoop merchandise from the shelves and into brown
paper bags. The store smelled of rubber and sugar. The shelves
were stacked to the twelve-foot ceiling with soaps, canned soups,
cereals, slacks, work shoes, nails, pencils, pads of widely lined

paper, glue, and candy. I distinctly remember the sound of doors: first the old metal screen door as it snapped closed behind us, followed by the rattle of bells as we forced the heavy wooden door open and stepped into the warm building.

In the early 1890s everyone shopped at Johnson's. Pictures from that time show tidy rows stacked in abundance. Store customers handed clerks written grocery lists with requests for ground coffee, bananas, and anything else they needed. The clerks happily filled the orders as (I suspect) neighbors stood in the aisles and talked. This was business in a small town.

Johnson's Store closed before I entered kindergarten. I rode by the building every morning on the bus. Each time I passed Johnson's I smelled the sugar and rubber and remembered the hardwood floors. The brick building seemed to be waiting for someone to turn the lock and pull up the shades.

As the years passed, the building began to sag. BB pellets and stones shattered the windows. Then one year I returned from college to find a gaping hole where Johnson's once stood. Imagine opening a magazine, turning to a full-page ad, but someone before you has ripped out a large image on the page. This was Johnson's: pieces of brick still clung to the edges of surrounding buildings, and a dark outline showed where sun hadn't shone for years, clues that something was missing. This happened again with the lumberyard and later with the Main Street Café.

Today many people refer to Wyndmere as a "bedroom" community, a "ghost town." There are bodies, people, but the center of town is empty—as hollow and sad as a gutted fish. During the day most of the gathering happens in Cenex, on the edge of town, near a highway that leads to the rest of the world. I've driven through town on my harvest retreat, but found few reasons to stop.

Am I partially responsible for this loss?

Today I'm on the hunt for a village with life, with charm, a place that sends a shot of whisky warmth into my veins. My hunt is likely to be a challenge, though. Riding to the farm with Mom one morning I asked her where I might be able to find a good cup of coffee in the area, a cute coffee shop or something of the like. She responded, "We can stop at Cenex. I think they probably make those fancy coffee drinks you like there." *God, I'm in trouble*, I sighed to myself.

This make-do-with-what-you-have attitude is how I grew up. We couldn't immediately get anything—ever. We couldn't just run out and grab something we forgot. A trip to a grocery store, after the two in Wyndmere closed, was thirty minutes away. So we either augmented what we had with ingredients from Cenex in Wyndmere, or waited until we could get to Wahpeton. This deprivation connected me to a way of life fading into extinction. Most of the people born in the United States today—notwithstanding economic means—will always know the option to call for takeout, or to run to the grocery store in a pinch, or to have immediate access to just about everything. But Chinese delivery still seems as wondrous to me as having Publishers Clearing House show up at my door, telling me I've won ten thousand dollars.

The next small town on my journey, Rutland, is supposedly different from those towns with vacant buildings. There is a woman, I've heard—one not raised on the prairie—who came from Oregon, took over the grocery, and built in its place the Rutland General Store. This new store, according to lore, is big, open, filled with groceries, antiques, and fabrics. The place has a café with yummy brunches and serves, on occasion, gourmet suppers for only thirty-five dollars.

I know of people who have stayed put in rural America, but stories of people who came to the prairie as adults, from another place, are rare. I'm sure there are thousands of people who moved to Fargo for jobs and I know many are currently pouring into Minot for work in the oil industry. But this woman, this enigma, didn't move to Fargo, she came to Rutland, population 220, and apparently built a store. This I want to see.

The paved road leading into Rutland cuts through three ponds. I notice how water laps the shoulders on both sides of my car. These ponds—as royal blue as unbroken jeans—are lined with cattails and surrounded by golden cornfields. It feels like I'm crossing a moat.

On the right, just as I enter Rutland, a big, round sign boasts that I've entered the home of the world's largest hamburger, 3,591 pounds, made on June 25, 1982. *Gross*, I think. I'm not sure what to make of the sign, but I guess it indicates hometown pride. Next I cross the railroad tracks and pass a grain elevator on my left. Then I see it: the Rutland General Store. The storefront is old-fashioned, with a movie-like red marquee jutting out of the brown building. Two rocking chairs are sitting on the front porch. I park, get out, and study my surroundings. A pickup goes by. The town looks tidy. And right before I walk in, I can't help but notice the name of the cross street, Gay Street.

I open the door. Bells jingle when I enter and about twelve men in their seventies and eighties—wearing caps and flannel shirts, and gray or tan work pants, some with suspenders, and all with mugs in hand—stop talking. Faces with watery eyes, white stubble, age spots, and thick glasses turn from an expansive round table and stare at me. Some continue sipping their coffee—seemingly uninterested but looking all the same. I smile like I'm saying "cheese" for a photo, thinking I should say something or introduce myself but realize that my standing here is delaying normalcy. I step forward, act like I know where I'm going, and feel great relief when the low rumble of the men's conversation starts back up.

I wander around, cautious and slow, like an animal exploring new territory. The store's ceiling is as high as a gymnasium. The walls are decorated with rustic doors, animal pelts, faded pictures, and pioneer-like dresses. There is a deli to my left, with pies displayed on the counter—like bottles lined up in a carnival shooting gallery—and colorful cupcakes overflowing behind a glass case. A convenience store to my right is stocked with snacks and supplies. The back of the shop houses a full fabric store, with bolts of material lined up like books on a shelf, a prism of colors and patterns against the store's bright yellow walls. Several women are sewing at a table. One woman, with an apron tied around her waist, walks around with bolts of fabric in her arms like she is wheeling around a dim sum cart. In a little station where you pay for your goods, a display case holds mementos that tell of Rutland's history. Back in the front of the store, near where the men are sitting, is a short counter with red barstools where you can order the deli items. From the deli a breezeway with hardwood floors and pine posts opens into the other side of the building, which houses a full café.

I grab a bag of chips, a bottle of water, and bring them to the register. The woman behind the counter is busy helping a crowd of high school girls that just came in. "Are you the owner?" I ask when I hand her my cash.

"No," she says. I want to ask her about the owner, the store, this creation in the middle of nowhere, but she is busy. More girls congregate behind me, shoving goods onto the counter. "Where do you live?" she asks.

"Minneapolis," I say, then offer, "I'm on a small-town tour today." She looks up, curious. "Which I organized for myself," I clarify, "to check out the towns around here."

"Well, then you should come back for Uffda Day," she says, handing me a flier, then moving on to the girls' stuff. "It's next Sunday, right here in Rutland."

"Okay, thanks," I say, resisting the urge to add, "You *betcha*." I grab my bag and study the flier on my way out.

The next Sunday I am back in Rutland for Uffda Day. People of all ages dressed in windbreakers, sweaters, and Carhartt clothing make their way from parked cars to the center of town, as if gathering for a big family picnic. All of the buildings, from the fire hall to the VFW to the senior center, are hosting activities today. There is the lefse-making station, which I plan to hit first, and there are also quilt displays, pioneer-cooking demonstrations, craft booths, and an antique car show. In short, I am surrounded by a host of activities I honestly have no reason to find interesting aside from the fact that I'm here, on my harvest retreat, with the zeal of a modern-day explorer.

When I get to the center of town I stop to watch and listen. Horses are pulling a buggy full of people down the street, the animal's hooves clomping like wooden blocks in elementary music class. Behind me accordion music floats out of the VFW when the door opens. Around me people greet each other as they start to line up for a parade.

The VFW, where I go to get my lefse, is filled with senior citizens sipping steaming coffee, their small bodies hunched over the tables like sunken soufflés. I settle in the long lefse line and watch women make the Norwegian pancake. The first woman rolls a ball of potato dough into a paper-thin saucer the circumference of a pizza pan. She uses a flat stick to lift the sheet of dough onto a griddle where another woman soon flips the lefse using her wooden stick. Everyone in line admires their technique.

After a short wait I am served a warm piece of lefse, which I smother with butter and sugar, then roll into a tube. When I take my first bite I look up and notice a man at the back of the line who used to be a bus driver when I was in high school. A tiny man, Oscar has the sweet face and voice of a *Wizard of Oz* munchkin. Years ago he drove our sports teams to neighboring towns on game days.

I haven't thought about Oscar since I left high school, but seeing him in line makes me feel like no time has passed. He is resting on a cane, wearing a suit with a small US flag pinned to the jacket's lapel. His formal dress for Uffda Day—the most casual of small-town events—warms me. I walk over and, before I can even say hello, Oscar squeals in delight, "Mel! Mel! What are you doing here?"

I explain that I'm back home visiting and thought I'd check out Uffda Day. He tells me he is still going strong, has twelve head of cattle even, which hardly seems possible for this small man with a cane.

After we visit and I am ready to say goodbye, Oscar asks me the dreaded question, "Mel, are you married yet?"

I nervously bobble my lefse. As much as I want to speak the truth, I can't, at least not fully, not here in the company of Rutland's senior citizen population.

"No, no—not married, not sure I will be," I say.

Oscar gets a twinkle in his eye, an actual sparkle, and puts his hands on my shoulders. "I know why!" he says, and raises a finger in the air.

I start to panic, thinking that right here at Uffda Day this munchkin is going to be the first person to call me out. I brace myself as he brings his lips to my cheek and whispers, "You're waiting for me!" He laughs and then gives me three kisses on the cheek. I relax and let out my own laugh—one of relief.

After saying goodbye to Oscar, I wander around for a couple of hours, feeling the joy of being out on a bright fall day in a bustling small town. This is how it may have been years ago, when people filled the streets of all the towns I visited on my small-town tour. This is how it may have been before things changed, before people left. And so when I finally drive away from Rutland, visions of abandonment and revival occupy my thoughts. I think of my hometown, the life seemingly gone, and Rutland, a community embracing the past and trying to hang on. Then I think of Minneapolis, the city, the concrete, the energy that lured me and other midwestern kids, the place I sometimes think holds me patiently, like a good friend or host, waiting for me to let go. And I realize that until I can look people like Oscar in the eye, and talk honestly and openly, the city will need to hold me for a long while.

The Boy

During my junior year, loss was always looming. Fear was always present. I knew I was going to lose Jessica to college shortly. And I knew that there was the remote possibility that she would, at some point, finally date a boy. If not her senior year, then next year, far away from me, in a place when we could no longer spend our hours after school together or wake up on the weekends to waves of Christian music.

At this point in my young life I couldn't comprehend change. Change was always happening, of course, but not in big and meaningful ways. Life seemed to be the same version of what it had always been, year after year. I did not yet know that love would come and go. I thought love was supposed to last forever. At the same time I knew, in a quiet place in my mind, that my love for Jessica was challenged. The clock was ticking. If a boy didn't take her, graduation would. And, as cruel fate had it, before graduation, *he* arrived.

His name was Jake. He wasn't, as expected, from Wyndmere. He lived on the other side of the state, in western North Dakota. Jessica met him a few years earlier in Bismarck, during North Dakota's hundredth anniversary. Her sister had been selected for the centennial marching band, which was made up of high school kids who marched in small-town parades across the state. Jake was a trombone player.

Jessica returned from a long summer weekend, when her family had visited her sister, humming with the delight of having met so many interesting people. "You have *got* to come with me next time, Melanie. It is so amazing that Tess is doing this." The band was a taste of something big for Jessica, something accomplished.

"I should have tried out for that band," she told me on one of our drives in the country. My feet were hanging out of the window. The prairie air was blowing on my face. "There is one guy in the band who is *my* age."

"I thought you had to be a senior," I said, remembering when she had come to me rattling off the information she had learned about the band.

"I know, you do, but they were short trombone players and this kid is amazing. A state award winner. You should hear him play." She turned down the radio so that she could tell her story. "When I was in Bismarck, Tess made him play for me. He shut his eyes and played this *hard*, complicated piece." She was transported back in time and visualizing the experience as she related it to me: "His hand hardly touched the slide, but it was moving. The slide was gliding."

"Hmmm," I said, not knowing what else to say. The heat of jealousy flooded my body, like a warm washcloth being placed on my chest.

Soon after, Jessica invited me to join her and her mom on a weekend trip to bring her sister, Tess, to Bismarck for a special performance. After a four-hour drive, Jessica and I sprawled on the grass of the capitol amid a sea of North Dakota families. That night we watched fireworks explode in the sky while the centennial band played on the capitol steps.

"You'll get to meet Jake when we go pick up Tess," she told me. I was hoping I would escape the experience of meeting the boy who had warranted such a reflective moment in Jessica during our country drive.

"Oh, yeah. That trombone guy?" I acted like I had to retrieve him from the darkest and most remote reserve in my memory, while in reality the image of him was at the forefront, ready to spring on me any moment.

"Yes, silly. Jake. Remember, the kid who is probably the best trombone player in North Dakota."

"Cool," I said, flat enough to raise an eyebrow, but not enough to warrant the question "What is wrong?" Somehow, surprisingly, I had avoided that question most of my life. I had trained my entire being to conceal my disappointments, my pain, my questions, my truth. Plus, the time he had to interfere was short, limited. We would pick up Tess. I would say hello. We would be on our way. Simple. Then we would drive to the other end of the state, the other end of the world, and Jessica would be on to something new.

After the fireworks stopped and the crowd scattered we drove to the Bismarck Armory to retrieve Jessica's sister. When we finally spotted her in the crowd she was standing next to a young-looking boy with dark hair and exceptionally long limbs. His face was round and innocent, with freckles and a wide smile. Not Jake, I thought: too soft, too understated. The boy spotted us and waved.

"Jake!" Jessica said in a delightful cheer.

He had peeled his starched band jacket from his torso and was wearing a white T-shirt. His legs looked official in stiff, striped, marching-uniform slacks.

"Hey, you!" Jake took three giant steps to Jessica and swept her up in a hug. It was apparent that he was warm, friendly, and uninhibited in a way farm boys were not. The two had clearly gotten to know each other better than I had imagined. Jessica responded with a gleeful laugh. When he released her she turned to me.

"This is my best friend, Melanie."

"Hi!" Jake said, while he reached toward me and gave me a hug. "I heard a lot about you when Jessica was here." I hugged him back, noticing that he was warm. Jessica looked at me with a proud smile, almost like a parent.

"I'm scared to know what Tess and Jessica told you," I said.

"Don't worry. They only told me that you are *quite* inquisitive."

"Yes, you better watch out. I'll know your entire life history if they let me at you."

"I'd be honored to share," he said, pretending he had a hat and cape and was about to bow. Jessica laughed.

"Since we are driving by Jake's house on our way home, I invited him to ride with us," Jessica's sister announced. "We'll just drop him off on the way."

"Great!" Jessica said. *Yes, great,* I thought to myself.

On the drive I sat in the front passenger seat next to Jessica's mom while Jessica, Jake, and Tess sat directly behind us, in the middle seat of the family Suburban. I tried to turn around, to engage, but after a while I couldn't take it anymore. Jessica was beaming and I could tell she was performing, telling stories, talking quickly, and laughing in a loud, unnatural way. When I felt tears come, begging for permission to exit my body, I announced to the back seat that I was going to shut my eyes for a bit, nap until we arrived. Jessica barely blinked at this. I closed my eyes, squeezed the pain back into my body, and rested my head against the window.

An hour later we arrived at Steele, North Dakota, and pulled up to a little white house on the edge of town. Jake's parents would have nothing to do with us scurrying off down the interstate. We would stay for tea, they insisted. While Jake's parents visited at the kitchen table with Jessica's mom, Jake showed the three of us to his bedroom.

It was a simple room with a bed, dark walls, a desk, a music stand, and several instrument cases on the floor. The trombone, I learned on our drive, was only one of many instruments Jake could play, though it was his favorite. His bulletin board was wall-papered with certificates of excellence, awards from music competitions, and the desk was covered with sheet music, black with dense notes, unlike the airy music with lots of white space we played in band.

"Play something, Jake," Jessica's sister said, probably noticing the sheet music herself.

"Oh. Yes! Please!" Jessica begged. "I've told Melanie that you are incredible."

"Well, I guess you better play." I felt the need to encourage him. "And you better do it before I get out my alto clarinet to show you up." They all laughed. I quivered.

"In that case, I *better* play something," he smiled, almost a habit of his, I noticed, and carefully picked up an older-looking trombone out of a case. He put the instrument together and stood in the middle of the room.

In band I didn't think much of the trombones. Most of the trombone players were boys and half of the time they were screwing off. When they played, their part was flat, like geese honking. However, when Jake started to play he could have very well been playing a flute or saxophone. The melody rose from his lips, light and powerful at the same time. We all vibrated in the tiny space.

Suddenly I understood exactly why Jessica had been so compelled to tell me a story about the trombone player she'd met. As she had described, his hand seemed to float, almost as if the slide was being moved by pure energy, not his touch. With each powerful puff of his I visualized millions of little bubbles popping in the room around us. When he hit his last note—the climax of his performance—my eyes rested on a cross that was nestled among the certificates on his bulletin board. I looked closer. The cross was on parchment paper certificate from what seemed to be a church youth group. Beneath the cross, in bold letters, it read:

I AM A CHILD OF THE LORD
I AM SAVED
Signed:
Jake Jerkins

I knew right then that I was going to experience an avalanche of sorts. I was going to take a hit. When the avalanche overcame me, I would try to stick my pole into any solid chunk of ice, try to keep from hurtling dangerously out of control.

I knew deep down that this goofy boy, this gifted trombone player, was going to be a problem. He not only brought out a terribly annoying and contrived side of Jessica's personality— she clearly wanted to impress him, I noticed, as she sat on his bed with a big smile, straightening her shirt and brushing hair from her face—he also shared my greatest connection to Jessica: God. The certificate on his wall suddenly made him dangerous. He was not a boy from Wyndmere. He was a Christian. He was viable.

On our drive home that night, in the very back of Jessica's parents' suburban, Jessica fell asleep on my shoulder. I didn't sleep. I stared into the dark night, watching the mile markers go by. The radio crackled with a talk radio station. Jessica's sister sat in the front. She and their mom exchanged words every thirty minutes or so, though I couldn't hear anything they said.

Why, I wondered, would a boy be better? I thought about this hard. Why would I have to step aside and watch a boy move into the space I shared with this person? The question was as elusive as a word problem. I understood the terms, but I couldn't get my head around the answer.

After that summer I didn't have to worry about Jake very often. He'd come up in conversation from time to time, but I'd brace myself and wait until the topic subsided. Then, during her senior year, Jessica qualified for the North Dakota All-State Choir. She went to Grand Forks for choir practice and ran into Jake who had, coincidentally, also made the choir. The two got reacquainted. When she returned from Grand Forks, Jessica received her first letter from Jake. His handwriting was neat and square, just like the handwriting I saw on his wall. The first card had a goofy duck on the front with a smile as wide as Jake's. On the inside it said, "Just wanted you to know someone is thinking about you." In his own writing he filled the first blank space of the card with paragraphs about school and his family. He wondered how she was and had decided to write, he said. Then in the last paragraph he wrote that God had placed Jessica *on his heart.* "We should try to get together this summer," he added. He signed it with *our* ending: In Him, Jake. I knew the avalanche I had dreaded years earlier had finally begun.

Jessica let me read the card. She let me read all of his cards, which then came quickly and frequently. And in his neatly prepared cards he started to witness to her, sharing his ideas about what it meant to him to be a good Christian. Jessica wrote back. They exchanged Bible verses and the names of songs. She bought music he recommended and played it on our drives down the gravel roads. My fear was becoming a reality. He was taking my place. They were—I thought as I read his letters—becoming like us.

I wanted to confess my feelings, but I couldn't find the words and I couldn't imagine her response. She already knew, I thought, anyway. She had to understand because she was living our relationship along with me. Talking to her would have been as odd as watching a movie with her, only to spend the entire drive home telling her what I had just seen, as if she had not been there.

A month before her graduation a letter arrived with the dreaded news.

"Melanie. He's coming. He's—actually—coming!" she said, her eyes bugging out.

"What do you mean, he's coming? Coming where?"

"To my graduation!"

"What! Did you invite him?"

"Well, yes. I sent him an invitation. But I never expected him to actually *come.*"

"Okay, what did he say?" I asked. She opened the card—they were always cards—and read.

"I'd love to celebrate your graduation and it would be wonderful to see Tess." She looked up at me with big eyes, as if to
say, "Are you hearing this?" and then continued, "And if it isn't
too much trouble, I'd like to come a few days early to spend time
with you. I know you'll be in the middle of finals, so please tell
me if it won't work. In Him, Jake."

"Mmmmm. Interesting," I responded, mustering up enough
intonation in my voice to sound at least neutral on the matter.

When the cards first started to arrive Jessica had asked me several
times what I thought of Jake. It was obvious that he had some
interest in her, since he wrote out of the blue to befriend her. She
also went so far as to contemplate whether or not she was attracted to him, in a meandering, thinking-out-loud way. "I don't
know, Mellie. He's sort of cute, I guess. And so talented. And a
Christian. He's like us, Mel." I would listen, falling inside, grasping for control.

What I wanted to say was, "He is *not* like us." But instead I
responded, "I'm not sure if he's right for you. He seems a little
boring. Who knows?"

I wasn't sure if he was the one, the one we had talked about,
the one we had imagined she would kiss. I wasn't sure what to
do or say. What seemed impossible—our separation—was happening and I certainly didn't know how things were supposed to
work, because everything that was supposed to happen didn't
make sense.

On the last week of school Jessica was busy and distracted, worrying about finals and working with her family to prepare for her
graduation open house. Each day she gave me updates about the
work they had done to get ready: they had cleaned the house,
mowed the lawn, planted flowers, ordered buns. I had planned to
go to her house on Friday to help.

Jake was scheduled to arrive on Wednesday night during the chaos. My heart ached, knowing he would be in the middle of the family activity while I would be home alone, working on papers that I could not, at this point, care less about.

My stomach felt like a wet glove, turned inside out to dry, when she approached me on Thursday morning in the hall. Her report, thankfully, was uneventful. The worst had not happened. Jake had arrived. They had all had supper and then Jake and Tess went for a walk while Jessica finished the last of her homework. *Her sister*, I thought to myself, *thank God*. I had all but forgotten that Tess and Jake were friends first. *She might distract him*, I thought.

"Are you going to kiss him tonight?" I finally asked, quite blatantly, in the parking lot, just before she was ready to drive home. I had to prepare myself. I had to know.

"I'm not sure," she said, looking into the sky and shrugging. "Maybe." Her response was more analytical than emotional, and it wasn't what I wanted to hear.

I could have, in that instant, grabbed her arm, forced her into my car, driven to a gravel road, and parked by a field to confess my feelings. I could have told her that for nearly five years my heart had expanded like a ripe grapefruit with love for her, only her. And that to kiss Jake would destroy our connection, would be a betrayal, and would ruin everything. I could have reminded her of the drives, the talks, the nights under the stars. I could have ripped the cross from my collar, threatening to never talk to her again, forcing her to contemplate for herself what a loss of our commitment to each other would mean.

I could have, but I didn't. We were kids in the middle of the prairie and I didn't have the words.

"Well, this will be quite interesting," I said instead, digging my thumbnail into my index finger, displacing my emotional pain, pulling out my humor. I could always make her laugh. "Oh, my God. *Please*, close your eyes. Please! Do not stare back like some sort of fish." She started to laugh. "Pretend that you are not an eighteen-year-old lip virgin, which we both know you are."

"Shut up!"

"No, seriously. Don't stare. And don't shove your tongue into his mouth or anything like that." I scratched my chin, as if I was thinking hard. "And try not to drool."

"Melanie!" she screamed, laughing now, begging me to stop.

"No, seriously, and if he goes for the boobs—well, thank God you've invested in those fancy bras."

"He's not touching my boobs."

"You never know—boys move fast."

"I doubt it. He's too much of a holy boy," she said. My thumb was starting to throb.

"I'll be in your first-hour study hall for the report."

"I don't know, Mel. Maybe there won't be anything." The earlier analytical stare had turned into a soft, worried, reflective face. I could tell that she wanted to talk, perhaps process. But I couldn't. I was done.

"And I'll be over after school too, to help you finish getting ready for your party," I said, backing away, moving to my car.

"Oh. Sure. That will be great," she said, now starting to walk to her car.

I turned, one last smile, and then walked quickly to the doors that promised privacy. I got in the car, turned the key, drove from the school, and cried the entire way home.

I assumed that we would find a way to be together. Even if we didn't speak about our feelings, we would still be "us." I would, we had already discussed, follow her to college. This decision wasn't about a relationship. It was about academics and opportunity. She needed to be the best and so when it came to school she had completely convinced me—after researching and comparing—that a small private Christian college would be best for both of us. Her list of reasons was endless, from the job placement opportunities to the square footage of the dorm rooms. I didn't question her wisdom.

—∽—

I prayed hard the night I left her in the parking lot. Wrapped tightly in blankets I stared out of my basement window and prayed that they wouldn't kiss. The dark night sky above the farm was the loneliest sky I had ever seen. My existence on this planet seemed almost cruel. I was sick with a despair that comes when you allow yourself to grow into another human. Too young, I did not realize how dangerous dependency could be. I also did not realize that the excruciating pain was temporary. Like a delicate garden from which Creeping Charlie was being pulled, I was experiencing something that would allow me more room to grow.

The next morning, the last day of school, I walked into study hall where Jessica was seated. She was wearing orange and erasing something on a piece of paper. The room was mostly empty because everybody had been excused to clean their lockers. Spring, I remember, was everywhere: the color of Jessica's shirt, the scent of the world being let in through open doors, people moving freely through the school, teachers boxing the contents of their desks. Spring on the edge of North Dakota always meant transition, change. People came out of the winter and started to commune with the world and each other.

This transition now seemed raw and cruel. I wanted the seclusion of Wyndmere High, the dark days of winter, the bells between classes, and the promise of Jessica handing me a note in the hall. Everything was changing in that bright, exposed moment. Spring was here and I couldn't stop it.

"Did you kiss him?" I knelt down by her desk. A response seemed unnecessary: when she looked at me I already knew the answer.

"Yes," she whispered, in a hoarse, tired voice. "Yes."

Floating toward the Light

This is what I remember.

I am on the bed. Samantha sits naked behind me on a footstool in the tiny bedroom. Her body casts a shadow on the ceiling. Terry, the other naked body, sits at the edge of the bed by my feet. A lamp fills the room with orange light. I imagine that I am night-skiing, wearing orange goggles, floating down a hill over a blanket of snow. Pearl Jam is playing on a dusty CD player hidden under discarded change and crumpled receipts. It is their second album.

Samantha seems to move in slow motion. Her thin arms cast shadows across the room as she rummages for a pack of cigarettes tucked in a pair of Levi's. The plastic wrap crinkles. I hear her breathe through her mouth when she pinches the cigarette between her lips and reaches under graded papers for her lighter. The lighter sizzles, and she sighs with relief, welcoming the black smoke into her lungs.

I am not looking at either woman. I am just watching the shadows. The smoke curls like fingers—like their fingers—reaching around my body, dancing around my head, trying, I am convinced, to reach into my eye sockets, into my ears, into any opening that leads to my soul. *No!* I scream, though I do not let my voice leave my body. Instead I brush the smoke from my face. It rises to the ceiling in a white cloud.

Terry pulls on her clothes, covering her large breasts, thighs, and stomach. She is not ashamed of her body, over two hundred pounds, a full woman. I hide my body under a thin sheet that managed to stay on the bed while the rest of the bedding slipped somewhere onto the floor.

It will take years before I don't need to slip my clothes off in the dark, convinced that my thighs are too large and my hips are too wide. It will take years to love my body. And so, at age nineteen, I do not move like these other women who move about the room, confident, breasts hanging in the orange light. I should do the same, I think, sit up with my breasts exposed, run my hands through my messy hair, grab a cigarette, act normal. Instead I find my T-shirt in a ball by my feet, pull it over my head, and sink against the headboard of the twin bed.

Pearl Jam repeats. I am not sure if it is for the second time or the twentieth. Samantha and Terry chitchat, like after a party when the hosts—who earlier ran around frantically to ensure that the lights were dimmed, the candles lit, the brie and strawberries placed just so—are cleaning up, moving slowly, with tired eyes.

I have sacrificed my body—I realized right then—to hold a woman's hand.

This is my first year of college. After Jessica left Wyndmere, my senior year of high school dragged by in a slow, painful progression. From the outside my year appeared to be a typical last year of high school. I went to prom, was on the homecoming court, and stayed involved in all of the activities that a year earlier I had done with Jessica. Instead of spending nights after practice driving around in Jessica's pasture, where we had parked, talked, and watched lightning storms move across the prairie, I spent time with my other friends, curled up in cold pickup beds, driving down gravel roads on moonlit nights, contemplating how our lives were about to change. Yet as I became more extroverted in some ways, I was also entirely more introverted. Though I had never spoken about my feelings, Jessica had at least been an outlet. My love for her was an expression. Our affection had been my comfort. But she was gone, and I was alone as I was early on when I sat in a tree by our little green house, with knowledge of love but no way to experience that love on the prairie.

"I know it hurts, honey, but you still have lots of friends." Mom tried to comfort me in my misery, assuming I was mourning all of my friends who had left. "We can barely get you to stay home the way it is. You're pret' near never around on the weekend! *And* your friends will still come home. Most of them are in Fargo, for goodness sakes. They're not dead."

"Mom, weekends are not *enough*. They are all *gone*. My life has completely changed! Why couldn't I have been born a year earlier?"

What I actually meant was, *Mom, I miss my friends, but I'll live. What hurts is that the person I love is gone and nothing will ever be the same.*

"Honey, are you saying your prayers? You just need to keep saying those prayers."

"I kno-o-w, Mom!" I said in a whiny, frustrated voice, dropping my head into my hands. I had already been on top of the God plan, first asking God to lead Jessica back to me, somehow, then—later—asking him to help me let go of Jessica and find someone who would understand me, someone who would love the gravel road drives, someone who would love nature, someone who knew and loved God. I had tasted the sweetness of a relationship bound by the love of God and couldn't imagine not having that in my life.

"This will pass, honey, believe me."

By the time I reached college, a year and a summer had passed between Jessica and me. She came home a few weekends and I visited her, but after each visit I ended up collecting my tears in a reservoir at the back of my throat until I was alone and they could wash through me. At first I had to endure her Jake stories, their talks on long walks, how they first started holding hands, moments kissing by his family's lake cabin. They had managed to see each other on long weekends. She was busy as she told me her stories, unpacking her clothes, straightening her room, laughing, then throwing herself on the bed by me, looking at me with her familiar eyes and white smile. "Crazy, huh?" she'd say, squeezing my arm before rolling off again to play a CD. She wanted to process all of this with me. She wanted to share, like we had shared for years.

Her relationship with Jake was short-lived. They had stayed in contact over the summer, but he was going to college in Grand Forks—a long enough drive from where Jessica would be to keep them distant. The threat of the boyish trombone player seemed almost trivial after her first few weeks of college. Jessica came home talking about new people, her classes, her professors, and her traveling Recharge group. Recharge was a small group of college kids who traveled on the weekends to put on plays and sing for Christian congregations throughout the Midwest. Jessica's group visited youth detention centers to hang out, play games, talk, and—of course—witness to the young residents.

She rarely asked about my life and often scolded me when I told her about my weekends out with my other friends. "Seriously, Melanie, I don't understand why you run around like that. There is *nothing* here."

When she returned home, I felt invisible. As Jessica moved about her room telling me what we were going to be doing that weekend, I grew silent. What, after all, did I have to report? What did I have to offer? I was living the year she had already lived.

At the end of our year apart, Jessica announced that she would not be returning home for the summer. Instead was going to work at a Bible camp in Colorado. She would not be reachable by phone or by an easy weekend visit. My letting-go process was slow, like returning to the same wall, day after day, to peel wallpaper. But somehow each day got a little better, and at the end of the summer I realized I had healed when I received one of her letters in which she wrote about a guy named Josh she had met at camp. He was a blond mountain boy who wore a red bandana and hiking boots, someone she could see herself with, she wrote. I knew something had changed, because, rather than cry, I folded her note, tucked it in a box, and pushed it under my bed.

My first weeks of college were promising. The sun was shining, flowers were still blooming. I missed the farm, but didn't know what to expect. I watched crowds of happy people move across campus in waves. The sheer magnitude of people gave me a sense of possibility. Surely I was not alone anymore.

What I was looking for, exactly, was not easy to put into words. I wanted to love someone driven by her love of God. However, if I wanted to love a woman, wouldn't I be a lesbian? And wouldn't that be a sin? I knew that being gay was in direct conflict with God's will. But what of my notion of love fueled by a connection through God? A word was missing. A word to define the most intimate, loving relationship—where emotion and spirit and connection through God were more important than sex. I would, I figured, eventually have sex with a man. But how would that physical act supersede the importance of my emotional and spiritual love for a woman?

I joined my own Recharge group and went to chapel on campus for Wednesday night communion. Communion night—with music and excitement—was what I had been searching for in Wyndmere: a place to be surrounded by happy, upbeat, and alive people who cared about God. At the same time I tried to make sense of God in light of what I was learning in my religion classes: that the Bible was a historical document, written by men, translated over the ages. I was starting to question, in little ways, the practicality of faith. And yet all of my questions were easily dismissed by the notion that faith couldn't be intellectually justified. God was the wind. God was the grass. God was.

Shortly into the school year I was walking from class with a friend when she grabbed my arm and pointed to a woman walking by a campus pond. "Hey, that girl over there? She likes *girls*," she whispered under her breath.

"Likes girls?"

"Yes, *likes* girls—*you know.*"

In that moment—through a thicket of moving bodies—my eyes settled on Samantha for the first time, standing by the campus pond. She was slight, thin, her cheeks almost hollow. She wore Levi's and a T-shirt, and slung a backpack over her shoulder. Her arms dangled like a runway model's, but unlike a model she didn't wear make-up, though her lips, nose, and cheeks were tinted pink, as if she was fighting a cold.

"Really?," I responded, realizing that my classmate was delivering a sliver of campus wisdom, something one should know, in the same way one should know the name of the football team's starting quarterback or that of the best English teacher.

"Ya, really," she said, pleased, I could tell, in the way gossipers can be, that I didn't already know. I peered over my shoulder and watched the new stranger disappear into the crowd.

After that day I studied Samantha on campus as if I was Jane Goodall tracking chimpanzees in the jungle. I found her to be ordinary, at first. She was just a project, an experiment, someone I would watch over the top of my book as she walked past me in the library. Or someone I would notice in the dining hall, between bites of a bagel and conversation with friends.

After a few weeks, I started to know her particularities. She had a hiccup in her stride, stood with her weight on her left hip, and started her days with wet hair. By the time the cool fall weather rolled in, I no longer found her to be ordinary. She was now familiar and my blood moved more quickly when she passed.

I met one other woman during this time who also "liked girls." She had short blond hair hardened by styling gel. Her flesh flowed over the waistband of her jeans when she sat at her desk. And she had a boyish voice that seemed to contradict her large breasts. Terry did not play the game I would later play with so many of my friends, the courting and trust rituals that came before any word of truth was spoken. I met her in sociology class and she befriended me instantly. I wasn't drawn to her in the way I might have expected to be drawn to the first lesbian I met. I had a clear picture of the connection I was missing in life and I knew instantly that she was not it. However, on one of our walks home after class, she made an announcement that suddenly aligned our fate in a very unusual way.

"You know, you need to meet my girlfriend," she said.

"You have a—girlfriend?" I asked, not sure how to engage, what words to use, how to act.

"Ya, she's great," she said in her gruff voice, unaware of my trepidation. "So cool. Her name's Samantha."

"Samantha?" I repeated the name I thought I had heard.

"Yes. Samantha. Samantha Barns. Do you know her?" She looked at me with the same questioning creases that appeared on her forehead when she asked questions in class.

I start to review what I knew about Samantha. I had never seen the two together. Certainly, their relationship wouldn't have escaped me in all of my weeks of careful consideration.

"Is she thin, kind of tall? Does she carry a red backpack?" I paused, careful with my facts. After all, what should I know about somebody I don't actually know?

Terry stopped and turned to me. "Well, how in the *world* do you two know each other?" She had this way of projecting her voice, as if she was giving a speech, not conversing.

"Oh, I don't *know* her!" I started walking, trying to act nonchalant. "I just know who she is. I've seen her around." I shrugged. "My roommate had a class with her or something."

"That makes sense. I think she would have told me about *you*." Terry was already nudging me, planting innuendo to crack someone who she probably thought was a scared, young, silent lesbian. I was not this, I thought, so I pretended to not understand.

"Um, how—ah—long have you two been together?" My own voice sounded strange, talking about two women.

"Fourteen days. I met her at the homeless shelter downtown. We both needed credits for our social work major. She slapped on the potatoes and I added the gravy."

They met off campus, I thought. Now the gap in my observations started to make sense.

"I'm super excited. It all seems to be going really well. Hey! Really. We should all hang out!"

"Sure," I said, though what I really wanted to say was, "Meet her? Are you crazy?" I couldn't fathom what it would be like to actually meet a person I had cast as a star in my own silent world.

"Perfect. We'll plan something for next week," Terry said when we got to the sidewalk where I turned to go to my dorm and she continued off campus.

I paused before returning to my room. The earth smelled like fermented apples and a faraway fire. I looked into the gray sky, past the clouds, and took a deep, painful breath. Not only was Samantha dating someone, she was dating a woman I had already decided I was nothing like. This was a disturbing reality, one that left me feeling more alienated than when I was completely alone with my thoughts.

The next week I followed power lines above my head as I walked to Terry's apartment on a foggy night. She lived directly behind an old church. The church had stained glass windows and bells that rang on the hour. On this night the church seemed ancient, almost haunted because of how the fog shifted around its structure.

A few minutes later I entered a large white house without knocking, as Terry had instructed, and walked up a tight-carpeted staircase. The door was open at the top and I quickly took inventory of the room, which had a futon, a TV, a kitchen the size of a closet, and a door that led to a bathroom. Terry and Samantha were sitting close on the futon, bathing in a mixture of smoke and incense.

Not getting up, Terry offered me a seat, which is where I stayed for the duration of the evening. Samantha was quiet at first. She sank into the opposite end of the futon and looked at me out of the corner of her eyes while Terry talked. Our new proximity to one another—me visible, an object she interacted with—made her unfamiliar.

They were young—I realize now—though at the time they seemed so much older than me, since they were both seniors and it was my first year at college. It was their youth, I think, that led them to touch each other as we carried on our conversation. They wanted me to see. Maybe they wanted me to react. And though I didn't—I sat still and acted unmoved—my stomach knotted like a blob of tripe.

Samantha relaxed after I had been there for a little while, though she avoided looking directly at me unless I was talking. Knowing it was my first year, they rambled on about everything they found wrong with our college: the controlling administration, the bureaucratic "bullshit," the Bible bangers. I wondered what they would think if I told them that I was in the midst of trying to figure out where God fit into my life or that I might just be—I now had a name for it—a Bible banger.

"Don't you agree?" Samantha asked, finally looking directly at me from where she was curled at the other end of the futon, her eyes glowing. I nodded, not yet knowing what I thought.

After that night, the three of us started to hang out frequently. They never knew I had studied Samantha, though I had confessed I was searching for love, and it was a different kind of love. Though I wasn't sure what that meant, I knew—and I told them—that it was not like anything I experienced or saw around me. What I didn't say was that this included them.

On the night it happened, we were at Samantha's apartment. She lived a few miles from campus in one of the buildings that looked like every other building in the city. Her place had tan walls, a kitchen—with black-and-white-checked linoleum—that opened to a living room, a bathroom with gold fixtures, and a balcony.

Early that evening Terry left to get milk. By this time I had deduced that there might be tension between the two of them and that this tension might involve me.

"She's scared to leave me alone with you," Samantha said, confirming my intuition, when the door closed.

"I don't get it," I responded. I still had an underlying attraction to Samantha, but it was more like a device to keep me breathing until I found someone else who could really understand me. I had no intention of letting either of them know about my dormant feelings. I knew by her words, however, that the two of them must have developed secrets of their own.

"Who knows? She's paranoid." The sarcasm in Samantha's voice did not match the steady gaze of her eyes. "Let's look at that book," she said, changing the topic. I jumped at this, not wanting our discussion to go any further.

"You guys are going to give me so much shit," I said. They had begged me to show them my senior book. They wanted to see my pictures of prom and homecoming, events they never took part in because their cynicism had developed years before they left high school. They too were from small towns, but their relationship to their past seemed pained, poisoned.

By this time I had started to forge my own new style. Rather than the clothes I wore in high school, I wore pajamas and stocking caps to class in the morning and jeans with flannel shirts at night. I still wore makeup, but less. So I knew they would delight in the pictures of me in my prom dresses, my hair perfectly coiffed, and my face painted in Clinique makeup, which Jessica had brought back from Fargo and instructed me to use. I would validate that the pomp and circumstance they had not participated in during high school was—as they suspected—a masquerade. Surely there were others like them, or others like me, roaming, disguised, in the small-town lands. I was the proof.

They wanted to see it. They treated me as their little pet, so that every new development, every layer revealed, solicited glee from my new masters.

Samantha and I went into to her bedroom to start looking at my book while we waited for Terry. I skimmed by the pictures of Jessica as fast as I could. I had carefully printed some of our favorite Bible verses under our pictures. I wasn't too excited to have them notice.

"No way!" Samantha kept repeating as she paged through the homemade scrapbook with her mouth wide open.

I jumped when the door finally slammed. "Hey. Where are you two?" Terry called. *Great, we're in the bedroom,* I thought. Samantha didn't seem to mind—she didn't take her eyes off of my book.

"You have *got* to see this," Samantha shouted back, not allowing suspicion to settle in the air. "Terry. Seriously. Get in here."

They sat, one on each side of me, on Samantha's bed. We paged through my book. I studied images of people I'd known since kindergarten and considered how they never really knew me. And at the same measure, I sat between two women who didn't know me either, but knew of private feelings I had never shared with anyone else.

"Look at your hair. No way!" Samantha laughed.

"Look at those basketball shorts. How could you play basketball? You're too short," Terry teased.

I partially enjoyed the banter and the attention, but also felt annoyed because I knew they could never understand my story in those pages.

After several minutes of laughing I could feel the weight of their bodies relax into me. This is when Terry leaned behind me, grabbed Samantha, and whispered.

"Hey! No fair," I said. "What are you two talking about? I'm showing you my book. You can't talk behind my back."

They ignored my fuss. "You know, you're just cute." Samantha reached out and touched my face. "Isn't she cute, Terry?"

"Sure is. Cute little Bible girl. Cute little prom queen."

"Shut up, you two!"

This is when it happened, when my life changed. When I could have stood up, walked out of the door, and carried all of my daydreams from the past nineteen years with me, safely untainted. Instead, I sat—maybe just for a minute too long, maybe just a bit too curious. Slowly they sank into the bed behind me, both of them lying down. They poked me, tickled me. "Knock it off," I said, laughing, until they pulled me back onto the bed. I lay still between them with my book on my chest. "I shouldn't have shown you two," I said, pretending not to notice that we were all on our backs.

Perhaps it is clear, in retrospect, what would happen right then. But in my world there was no possibility I would have sex with a woman, and no way—ever—that I would have sex with two women at once. So when they started to kiss, reaching above me, so that their lips were in front of my face, I assumed that it was like the night I first met them, when they took pleasure from shocking someone who wouldn't tell because I was—they knew—guilty by association.

When Samantha turned and kissed me, I entered a strange coma, as one might enter if having a near-death experience, where one actually experiences something that one has heard about, but still thinks it can't possibly be happening. My ignorance could have been my worst enemy. I couldn't stop something that wasn't possible. When their hands started to tug at my clothes, when their lips started to brush mine, I didn't step out. Instead I floated toward the light.

After it was all over and they had their smoke, Samantha crawled into the bed and slid up next to me. Terry stood up right then asked Samantha to follow her to the bathroom. They returned a few moments later.

"We've decided that you can—*should*—sleep with us tonight. I mean, we're all friends here, and we don't want you to have to sleep on the couch," Terry said, though I could tell she was less than pleased with what she was saying. I went to the bathroom, looked at myself in the mirror, not sure who I was looking at. When I returned, the three of us crawled into Samantha's single bed. When Terry started to snore, Samantha reached over Terry's body and grabbed my hand.

When they both fell asleep, I watched a movie in my head. It seemed like I was watching the story of someone else. In this movie I see Terry and Samantha who are like wolves as they creep over my flesh. I do not move as they hover over me. Instead I lie on my back, as if I am in a casket, while they shift with instinctual purpose, changing positions. This is all familiar to them, the way people move during sex. Their bodies form constellations above me as they connect at different joints and form new patterns. I watch through squinted eyes. At the end, though, I do move slightly. I reach for Samantha's hand, which is at my waist, and hold it. Whenever she lets go—when the bodily constellation shifts—I search for her hand and secure her grip.

Perhaps I could have escaped back into the world the next morning without looking back. Maybe if I hadn't paused, if I hadn't thought about the night, I would have been able to leave that apartment unscathed. Instead my tears started when I reached for the front door. Sobs followed. I sank to the ground and started cry. I could not move.

Terry and Samantha led me to the bed and tried to comfort me. I didn't want them around me. I slammed my head against the wall, pulled at my hair. My mind filled with images. Faces, at first the size of quarters, growing until they were large, round saucers, seemed to be flying at me. They dissolved right before they reached me. The first face was that of my grandpa; the next was my grandma's; then came the faces of my brothers, my sister, my mom, my dad. They started to pick up speed, rushing toward me, giant heads looking at me. I screamed. I wanted to reclaim my body. I wanted to go back to who I was before they touched me. My parents would die, I thought, if they knew what I'd done. The entire town would gasp. I had done something completely evil. I wanted to kill the wolves that had feasted on me the night before and retrieve my carcass from their bellies.

Terry and Samantha held my arms, I struggled. I wanted to leave the bland walls, the colorless world. You can't leave, they told me, their words echoing in my blurry head. You're freaking out. I could not cry hard enough. I could not produce enough tears to flush my stained body.

When the faces stopped rushing toward me, I cried a slow and sad cry. Then I said, "I need to go," now calm enough to convince them I could leave.

I am not sure how this turned into trauma for me, but it did. Surely this is what kids do—go to college and experiment with sex or drugs or other rites of passage. Years later I would spend many late nights laughing with friends as they proudly confess details of their latest trysts or sexual escapades over wine and garlic-infused dinners. "You did *what?*" We will cackle and laugh, some of us prudes, some of us open. We will discuss the boundaries we have meandered along and the pain and pleasures we've reaped with our choices. We will marvel at those who can hold polyamorous or monogamous relationships in ways we can't comprehend. We will talk, on these nights, of the complications of relationships and commitments and love and sex. Gender will blur, hardly mattering anymore.

So, perhaps on that night what was lost to me had less to do with my body than with a simple childhood daydream. Perhaps on that night I began a lifelong mourning process for the perfect, knowing love I carried with me for so many years. Perhaps I encountered the first of many sobering lessons that love and sex will rarely converge, that love will take many forms, certainly, and will lead me on many journeys, but it will rarely find me in uncomplicated, ideal ways.

On that morning, as I left the apartment, I don't know any of this. All I knew as I stepped into the parking lot was that I was angry at its ugly, expressionless asphalt. *Nobody cares that this parking lot is so ugly and flat*, I thought. *Nobody cares about the unsightly garbage bins, collecting the disgusting leftovers from the rest of the wolves.* I looked up at the building, the uniform balconies, lined with tiny Weber grills and baby strollers. I was angry at this too. Rage filled me, knowing that people can be so stupid, so content to live inside the ugliness of tan walls.

Redheaded Redneck

"**I**f you want to know anything about North Dakota or farmers, you should really talk to Joel Heitkamp," Mom says, moving about the kitchen, munching on a snack and cleaning up. I'm at the kitchen table, writing. I just told Mom about Rutland and Uffda Day. "Joel's one of those sort of people who knows a lot about politics. But that isn't all he talks about. You can talk to him, not know much about that political stuff, and not feel stupid."

"I guess that's comforting," I say, continuing to write as she goes on.

"He talks to farmers all day long. He'll have something interesting to say." She grabs the phone book from a drawer and pages through. "Here, call him." I look uneasily at the number she has scribbled in pencil and stop what I'm doing.

"You just want me to call his, ah, house?"

"Yes. He's a really nice guy," she says, ignoring my trepidation.

Since being home I've learned all about Joel. He is one of voices on the radio in the shop, mingling with the sound of welding, air compressors, metal clanging, and trucks moving into the yard. He's on KFGO, the Mighty 790, based in Fargo. Joel served in the North Dakota legislature for fourteen years and is the successor to Ed Schultz, who used to be the host of the show *News and Views*. Ed grew beyond his North Dakota britches and now has a nationally syndicated radio and TV show. So Joel is here, holding down the Midwest fort.

I've gotten in the habit of listening to Joel in the morning, even when I'm not in the shop with Dad. Joel covers topics from crop insurance to proposed measures on the upcoming ballot, from updates about the oil boom in Minot, to interviews with political figures or finding the best hamburger in small towns. He has the classic voice of a radio host: kind, dynamic, and engaging, with a bit of a salesman's bravado mixed in.

Listening to Joel is like having a play-by-play of harvest too. Soybeans are finished, everyone is on to corn. The weather is warm, the land has dried, prices and yields are high. Dad thinks they'll be done with corn by the end of October, a record. The state's farmers are experiencing a bumper crop, apparently, and—as odd as I would have found this a couple of weeks ago—hearing farmers call in and share harvest updates from across the region makes me feel like I'm in the heart of something big.

It feels weird to call, but I remember that this is how things operate back home and punch in the number. Besides, I tell myself, Joel does seem like the perfect person to talk with on my harvest retreat. He's here, immersed in the people, immersed in their conversations. He might help me understand why I was drawn back to this place or why I left in the first place.

"This is Joel." His jovial voice immediately puts me at ease. After I explain that I'm home for harvest and am interested in what he might have to share about living here, he tells me he'd be thrilled to talk with me and to call him next week when he's back in town. Later on the radio I hear he was in DC when I reached him, picking up the Marconi Radio Award given by the National Association of Broadcasters for small-market radio station of the year.

"Is he famous?" I ask Mom.

"Oh, I suppose he's well-known around here," she responds.

Next week, I pull up to Paula's Place at four-thirty in the afternoon. Paula's is a bar and restaurant in Mooreton, population 204. There are two other cars parked on the street. Most everyone in the county is in the field harvesting corn.

While I'm still feeling odd about this meeting, I'm looking forward to a beer. A few hours earlier I visited the farm to see what Dad was up to and if I could help. I sensed immediately that things were not going smoothly. Dad was studying the appendage of a grain cart; everyone else was pacing around the yard. While I haven't been around the farm for harvest in years, lessons from childhood stick: Tension up? Lie low. I whispered to my cousin, "This an emergency situation?"

"Yup," he said. Something on the grain cart is broken and the dryer has not been working properly, I learned.

After a bit of walking around, studying the scene, I found the courage to approach Dad. "Something broken, Dad?"

He looked down from a stepladder he'd positioned near the grain cart. "Yes, can you tell what it is?" he asked, as if to say, "You think you could be a farmer, huh?" I studied the thing he was tinkering with, which looked like a blade or a fan in a long cylinder.

"Ah, is that fan thing not turning properly? Hitting the side?" I hypothesized.

"No," he huffed and shook his head. "This piece busted." He pointed to a stub that I wouldn't have known was not in its entirety. "This runs into here and turns this." He traced the air to show me the purpose of the missing piece. I was trying to follow the "here" and "this" but was confused.

He tells me later that the drive mechanism that turns the auger when it folds over onto the grain cart was broken. And because the mechanism was broken it wouldn't move the grain though the auger. I thank him for the information, having no idea what he'd just said.

Looking up at Dad troubleshooting the problem, his earlier words came back to me: "Farming's fun until something goes wrong." I decided it best to not bug Dad for another assignment right then. Instead, ignoring my innate rebellion against stereotypical roles, I cleaned up the dishes from lunch scattered around the shop kitchenette until it was time to go meet Joel.

—⚊—

Paula's is empty and still. A Milky Way of dust floats in a light beam that is shining onto a small corner of the bar. The rest of the place is dark. I assume a man sitting at the bar with his back to me is Joel. When he turns I recognize him from the picture on his website.

"Joel? I'm Melanie." I walk up to him and extend my hand.

"Hello!" Joel gives me a warm, welcoming handshake. Even if he has no idea why he's sitting here, I know Mom is right. At the very least, I don't think he'll make me feel stupid.

"How long do you have, Joel?" I ask, wanting to be respectful of this man's time.

"Let's see. The Twins and Yankees play at seven," he says. "I'm good till then."

Joel asks me if I want a beer, which I do. As I settle, sip my beer, and take out my notebook, Joel tells me he grew up in Mantador and served in the North Dakota legislature. Details I know through Mom. I study him while he talks. He has red hair and a solid build and is wearing casual work clothes, khakis and a polo shirt—he must be on his way home from Fargo, where he hosts the show.

I explain to Joel that I'm home to understand why I'm drawn to rural America and that Mom thought he'd be a perfect person to talk with, since he talks all day long with people who live here. "So," I ask Joel, "tell me why you live here. Why you stay."

He's thinking, but his response doesn't take long. "I have seven siblings, and we were all born in nine years. Six of them still live here. And the one who doesn't live here, we talked twice already today. You know, family is important."

I think about my family and understand what Joel means. It is so simple, really, our connection to people who "know us." At the same time this connection is also what I've avoided over the past several years.

"Makes sense," I say, and fill him in on my family configuration. He knows Mom and Dad's generation, my uncles and aunts, but he isn't familiar with my siblings or me.

We talk some more and then I think to ask, "You know, when I travel I find that people are sincerely surprised that I am from North Dakota. Do you ever experience that?"

"Oh, man. All the time!" Joel laughs. "Their first impulse is that North Dakota is cold and we have yearlong winters. I never lie to them." Joel shakes his head with conviction.

"Yes—I think Minneapolis is even milder than it is here," I add.

"We've had winters that start at Halloween and that extend to Easter and beyond. So I never try to make North Dakota what it's not," Joel says. "But we've had friends come from all over the United States, and we've had exchange students, and everybody loved it here and wanted to come back. This place is a little hidden treasure, in my mind." Joel thinks for a minute and continues, "But I'm not a big believer that all parts of North Dakota are beautiful. Farmers are planting less shelterbelts. We're flat. You go into some of our small towns that are hundred-plus years and they're going downhill. We could lie, we could say, 'Oh, my God, there's nothing like a wheat field.' The truth of the matter is the strength of North Dakota is in the people."

Over the years I have mourned the loss of the shelterbelts, the familiar clusters of trees that framed the fields and protected the land from erosion. As a child I'd enter into those woods like the children in *The Lion, the Witch, and the Wardrobe* wandered through the wardrobe to discover Narnia. Most of my favorite groves are now dying and rotted. The changing landscape saddens me, but in a state where grasses are native to the prairie soil, trees won't thrive without the attention of farmers.

"Speaking of people, how would you describe the North Dakotans?" I ask.

"Well, if you walk to my car parked out front right now, you'd find the doors open and the keys in it," Joel says and pats his pockets to show they are empty.

At this point a woman in her fifties or sixties, with short hair and glasses, wipes the counter in front of us. "Paula, I'll have another beer," Joel says. "Paula is my niece's mother," he explains to me.

"Your niece-*in-law's* mother," she corrects him like a schoolteacher, giving him a playful smile.

I laugh because we're sitting in this small town, in Paula's— and this is Paula, who, of course, shares a relative with Joel. She looks at Joel's wad of cash lying on the counter. "I'll wait to collect because you're buying her another one," she says and points to me. I like this woman.

As Joel and I talk, I remember that I'm sitting with a practiced politician, someone who knows the ins and outs of politics in rural America. Growing up, I was completely unaware of the political context of my small town. The only politics I was privy to included stories about who was overbearing on the Crop Show committee. And my parents seem to be friends with everyone and anyone, regardless of political affiliation. I explain this to Joel and ask, "Is this typical?"

"Oh, yes. It's almost rude to talk politics," Joel says, taking a drink of his beer. "Well, on our talk show, you can *talk* politics as long as you don't mention a party. It's like the debate between Catholics and Lutherans. People can say they go to Saint John's, but not Saint John's *Catholic church*. North Dakotans aren't afraid to talk politics, as long as you don't say *what* you are. I'm going to show you something that gets at what you and I are talking about." He grabs a notepad and holds it up. Three names are listed on the top. "They're all running for the North Dakota state legislature. What party are they from?" he quizzes me.

"I have no idea," I say, the names are not familiar.

"Exactly. You're not going to know unless you get out your cheater glasses." He moves his palm to show me, in tiny print at the bottom, a Republican endorsement.

"What other state do you see that in?" he asks. "And two of these guys I count as good friends," Joel says, making this point because he is a Democrat.

"What party is more favorable for the plight of farmers?" I ask, wanting to know from the expert.

"The Democrats!" he says, like "Hello, ask me a hard question." His answer does not surprise me.

"Okay, then why are so many farmers Republicans?" I ask, knowing the state is tipped toward the red.

"Who do you cheer for in major league baseball?" he asks. The answer to this is actually no one, but I get where he's going.

"The Twins." They would be the only team I'd watch in the World Series.

"And who do your parents cheer for?"

"The Twins."

"There you go. Besides the fact that I believe what I believe, my mother was a progressive," he says.

"*My* mother sat on the election board with his mother. She was nonpartisan," Paula says, cracking open a beer and setting it down in front of me. "She'd wear a donkey on one side of her glasses and an elephant on the other during Election Day."

"If you drive by Paula's father's house in Hankinson right now, he's got every Republican sign on the lawn you can imagine. But when I ran, he'd put my sign in his yard with all of the Republicans," Joel laughs.

Paula pounds her hand on the bar and lowers her voice into a curmudgeon's growl, mimicking her father: "He's the only goddamn Democrat I'd ever vote for!"

"So," Joel points at Paula, "that's North Dakota. We're incredibly loyal."

"Speaking of loyalty," Joel says, "I think one of the biggest tests for North Dakotans was when the ELCA came out allowing openly gay ministers to serve. That was a huge issue. For the first time ever, North Dakotans are having to acknowledge what the rest of the country has, which is, we have children and siblings and family members who are gay."

I'm totally taken aback by this but I nod my head, letting him know I agree with him, letting him know I'm not against gays or anything, even though I'm from North Dakota. He sips his beer and continues.

"Just a while ago, not too far from here in rural Minnesota, someone wore a rainbow to communion—you know, a gay symbol." I nod. "And the Catholic church refused to give communion to this person. So to pretend we are at the cusp of changing society—" He shakes his head in disbelief.

"Yup," I say, fascinated with this dialogue. I want to hug this self-described 230-pound redheaded redneck.

"I'll tell you, I came out on air and said the worst vote I ever made in the legislature was based on reelection. I voted to ban gay marriage in North Dakota. I promised myself if I did run for higher office I wouldn't run and lie. So I said that was a stupid, asinine vote and that I'd voted to cover ass rather than my conviction," he says, taking another swig.

"Really? What did people say?"

"Oh, you'd be surprised at the positive response I got from people who sent me e-mails but just didn't want their names on air. It is exactly what we're talking about," Joel says. "As long as you don't speak it, you're okay."

"Well, I happen to be gay," I say, pretending Joel doesn't know everyone in the entire county.

Joel's eyes widen and he holds his hands to his chest. "Really? I honestly had no idea."

"Yes, that's part of the reason I don't live here," I say, shocked at my bravery. Under normal circumstances my heart would be beating wildly, leaping out of my neck like a salmon heading upstream to die. But something about Joel puts me at ease. It is probably his directness, which makes me feel like I'm not in a small town but at a bar in the city where my admission would barely cause me a second thought.

"I don't blame you, actually," Joel says. "I think we are about twenty years away from acceptance. My daughter's generation will be a lot better at letting people in, rather than finding ways to hold them out."

At first I'm relieved, hearing that Joel thinks the next generation could be more accepting. But then I'm uneasy, because I know my fear, my paranoia, is not totally unfounded: Joel hears these people, Joel knows these people, and whatever he hears and whatever he knows leads him to not *blame me* for my departure. Still, as we continue our talk, and eventually progress to other topics, I can't help but think how Joel shared, unprompted, his opinion about what's right, what's just, not caring, really, how I might have responded. He's just taught me a lesson.

After some moments, I decide to delve deeper. "Joel—so, about people not talking, I grew up not talking about my feelings. I partially attribute my silence—rightly or wrongly—to being from here, to growing up around North Dakotans who avoid talking about their deepest feelings. But you talk to people from here all day long—it's your job. What do you think?" I ask him, not sure what I'm really getting at.

"Well, like I said. If you avoid the controversial things, if you avoid controversial topics, like 'Harriet's a drunk,' it's a wonderful place to be."

"And do you think avoiding topics is a good thing or bad?" I ask.

"Bad," he says, taking the last swallow of his beer. "Bad."

Paula zips by us then, explaining that she needs to run home and make popcorn for one of her regulars. The bar's popcorn maker is broken and she hasn't had a chance to fix it, we learn—but this customer loves his popcorn and he's on his way. *Now that's loyalty*, I think.

While I watch Paula gather her things, I think about how in this land we may conceal parts of our lives that make others uncomfortable, but—darn it—we're loyal.

Bible Camp

If there is one place a young woman probably shouldn't go after a first year of college marked by a sexual encounter with two women, it is probably Bible camp. Even so, the summer after my first year I decided to follow Jessica's lead one last time. Pictures that covered bulletin boards in many dorm rooms moved me: people browned by the summer sun, wearing backpacks, their arms around each other, with mountains behind them and wildflowers at their feet. I needed to reclaim my purity, somehow. I needed to be like the light-hearted, devout, Jesus-loving kids who I saw in those pictures. I needed to be who I had been before the wolves.

Jessica had worked at a Bible camp in the Colorado Rockies. She had returned pontificating about land conservation and how God doesn't have a gender, and talking about her weeklong treks into the mountains. Interested in this new way of understanding God, I too intended to go to Colorado, where I would spend my summer in hiking boots, learning how to survive in the backwoods. When the camp acceptance letters came, however, I did not get one from Colorado. Instead, I received a letter from a camp in Iowa.

A month later I stepped out of my car and onto a flat, half-empty parking lot. There were people in the distance on a small hill, walking amid a bunch of nondescript brown buildings. I was not in the mountains. I did not see wildflowers and I certainly would not need a backpack or hiking boots here. Still, I knew the camp was on a lake, and the lake was probably somewhere behind the buildings. The lake would be my first destination, I thought.

Like at the farm, I would connect with the land and then find people. But before I even had time to feel lost or unsure of what to do next, I heard a voice.

"Ah, you're here! Welcome! Welcome!" A woman was moving toward me, walking like a speed walker in a mall, with her hand up in the air. When she was nearly to my car she stopped as if she had forgotten something, bent down, looked at my license plates, and then continued to me with open arms. "Well, well. Good ol' North Dakota. Long drive, huh?" Without missing a beat she hugged me as if she had known me for years. Still holding my arms she backed up and studied my face over her glasses. "My name is Catherine. I am the camp director. Welcome."

Catherine was cheerful in the way you would expect the Bible camp greeter to be when you first arrive. I, on the other hand, felt awkward. I reached out, though, and hugged her as I might hug a distant relative.

"I'm Melanie," I said.

"*Melanie*, we are so glad you made it," she said, articulating all of her words very carefully.

"Come now. Let's grab your belongings and I'll show you to the dorm." I opened my trunk and we both grabbed my stuff.

"Several of the girls are already here," she said. "All of the girls will be rooming together in the bunk rooms until the campers get here."

I took inventory as Catherine and I walked toward the camp. I saw what looked like three dormitories or apartment buildings. Farther ahead, I could see a line of cabins on the lake. In the middle of the small campus, there was a dining hall and gym. And at the top of a hill was a building with a big cross. "That's the chapel," Catherine said, noticing my gaze.

Catherine guided me to my room, where a couple of girls were already organizing their clothes and emptying their bags. We exchanged introductions and I placed my things on one of the bunks.

"You gals come find me if you need anything. Okay?" Catherine smiled, satisfied that she had led me to my quarters. "I'll be up at the main office, just down the hill," she said as she turned to leave. Before she had completely stepped through the door she paused and turned back to us.

"God is going to do wonderful things this summer. God is so good, isn't he?" Her eyes were wide—a cheerleader for God. Her curious behavior startled me a bit, but then I realized that this must be part of her job. She didn't wait for an answer before she stepped out of the room.

Jill was one of the girls unpacking her bags. She was tall, with long brown hair, and wearing jeans and a tie-dyed shirt. She took control of the room, talking to me and another girl named Cheryl as if we already knew each other. Cheryl was the opposite of Jill: short and round, with rosy cheeks and blond hair cut neatly to her chin.

Together, Jill and Cheryl are classic examples, as I quickly learn, of the two kinds of kids camp attracts. The first group is comprised of the church kids, who have been good their entire lives. Some of the church kids have a father or grandfather who is a pastor, PKs they are called—short for pastor's kids. The second group is comprised of rebels. Many of the rebel kids are on a journey to seek forgiveness or redemption. The rebels, like Jill, either grew up with God and then took a major detour in life, or they never considered God until they'd had a late-night talk in the dorms where someone shared how they accepted Jesus Christ into their lives. As is their nature, the rebel kids are open to trying anything once, even God.

Several other people joined us as we unpacked. I knocked them off in my head—church girl, rebel girl—classifying them the best I could as they shuffled through layers of their belongings, which become little clues to what these people might be holding close, hiding, carrying into their summer, similar to how I carried a secret into mine. I studied and quickly categorized the dozens of people I met in the first few days at camp. As easily as I thought I could place everyone into a category, I did not think anyone fit into mine.

After the night with Samantha and Terry I walked around on campus with a blank face. I didn't *see* anybody. I was depressed and lonely. Nothing comforted me. I spent some time with Jessica, but we were different people and she now lectured me about hanging out with weird people. "I don't get it. You have these new, bizarre friends. I don't even know you anymore." The truth was, she didn't. I was in my first relationship with a woman and she had no idea.

Samantha left Terry. Shortly after they broke up, Samantha and I began dating. At first I didn't want anything to do with either of them. But Samantha called me, wanting to talk. I agreed to meet her at the Fargo Frying Pan for coffee, at first just wanting her to know how much I hurt. As we processed the night, she never seemed to understand what the big deal was. Because she was the closest I had to a witness, I started to dismiss the entire event myself. I just shut it off and pretended it didn't happen.

The only reason I entered into the relationship with Samantha, I think now, was to somehow justify what I had done. If she could turn out to be the person I had been waiting for, the love I had been searching for, maybe the night where I sacrificed my body would make sense. Maybe my pain would leave.

At dusk I sat on campus, often by the pond where I first saw Samantha, and tried to remember God. He seemed so far away, no longer real. I desperately needed to be told I was okay, that I was forgiven, that I wasn't going to hell. This need, greater than any I had ever felt, drove me to visit the campus pastor. I didn't plan to tell him about the wolves. But I did plan to tell him that I had feelings for women. I thought that the pastor would know, as all true believers did, that my feelings weren't really evil. I thought he might let me into the secret that while it was his job to tell people that gays were sinners, the real truth was that this was just an old church line. And that the kind of love I was seeking was indeed angelic, pure, holy.

I scheduled an appointment during the pastor's office hours. A sign invited anyone to sign up. I immediately regretted sitting down in the big leather chair in the small office, a few feet away from the man I had seen only in chapel, up on a stand, preaching to hundreds of kids. Now I could see his pores and I knew somehow that he would not be delivering the message I wanted to hear.

When he started talking, telling me about how true Christians "separate the sin from the sinner" and how I really needed to understand the danger of "homosexuality," his words started to blur. I wanted to run out of his office. The more he talked, the more I saw parts of me falling away in his eyes. I was no longer whole.

When he finally stopped talking he placed his pencil next to his temple, as if contemplating something deep and profound, but his eyes were empty. I told him I would think about what he said, then I thanked him and left.

That semester a former nun taught my religion class. She challenged the class to read the Bible using critical thought and historical analysis. To my surprise the nun argued with students who were horrified at the suggestion that the Bible might be a metaphorical interpretation of myth, and not absolute truth. While I should have been on the side of the kids, I found myself rooting for the nun. Her ideas allowed me to retain some connection to God, to peel God away from his leaders and his people, most of whom—I was learning at school—condemned gays. Her words helped me believe that maybe, just maybe, these people might not have full rights to God's story. Maybe there was something less black-and-white to consider. This inclination allowed me to hang on to the wave of peace I felt by the pond or in a moment of quiet, a peace that was harder and harder to feel in church.

I was dealing with a powerful paradox: I was either condemned to hell for being gay—or the God I had known, wrapped up in all of the Bible stories I'd learned, was not exactly as I had believed.

—ɯ—

My first evening at Bible camp we congregated in a room by the cafeteria where a small group of returning counselors and permanent staff welcomed those of us who had just arrived. If I could have walked out right then, I would have. Everyone was talking. Conversation was buzzing around me, just out of my reach. I swallowed my discomfort, but it didn't leave. Instead it settled like a stone on the center of my chest. I paged through a red folder filled with handouts, looking busy, as if I was *choosing* not to talk, as if I was some sort of overachiever who'd heard a directive nobody else chose to follow.

As the new voices around me rumbled, a girl walked through the door and caught my attention. I looked up from my folder to watch her enter. She had long, blond hair, brown eyes, and a wide, full mouth. She was dressed in jeans, with a long T-shirt and a beaded necklace. Her energy was confident, though softness seemed to surround her. I instantly wanted to *be* her, wanted to be moving through the room, looking natural and generating warmth. The stone in my chest dissolved. *May.* I heard her name as someone greeted her. She stepped around several bodies and took the space right next to me.

"Hi. I'm May." Her smile loosened my discomfort and I quickly took note of how I too might introduce myself to others, following her lead.

"I'm Melanie," I responded, thankful to be saying something. I knew that May and I would become friends. But unlike with Jill, whose rebel story I could already tell, there was something different about May. This difference was less obvious, but more critical. I had a feeling that she, like me, was looking over the crowd, not taking the moment at face value, but searching for an answer, looking for something that might help her determine what her next steps in life might be. At the end of the summer, her story will remind me what I learned in my tree at age four. Life is never what it appears to be.

—∿—

"Okay, gang." Catherine got the attention of the crowd, not allowing May and me to say another word to each other. "As you'll all find, fellowship, singing, and praising the Lord will be a big part of our time together this summer," Catherine said, beaming with that same cheerleader shine I saw earlier in the day. "We're going to open with a song tonight, praising God for bringing us together. Praising God for being such a loving and *awesome* God," she glowed. "We're going to be seeing a lot of change this summer. We're going to be meeting a lot of lost souls who need our help. God is going to work through us to reach a lot of hurting kids," she paused, letting the words sink in. "I'd like to start by thanking our Lord. Let's join hands."

I looked into the circle. I could tell those who had been here before. They had an almost seductive smile on their lips, staring into the distance, seemingly at something I could not see. A few of them rocked back and forth, whispering, "Praise God" with their eyes closed. All of a sudden, while I was looking around, a voice rose out of the crowd. Others joined then, singing a song I knew from chapel at college.

> Our God is an awesome God. He reigns from Heaven above, with wisdom, power and love. Our God is an awesome God.

The room filled with the vibration of forty voices harmonizing. The song repeated, and this time we broke into rounds. Layers of voices filled the room, filled my chest, replaced my anxiety.

My body vibrated with a love I had felt in my childhood, a rich, maternal love. Suddenly tears filled my eyes. It was as if I was under the spell of a snake charmer. Visions from the previous twelve months flooded my mind. *I am a sinner. What have I done?* I closed my eyes, and—for the first time in a long time—did not hide my tears. This love is the truth, I thought, whatever *this* is, I must follow it.

We started our prep days in the chapel with a program led by the training staff. Mornings included a skit to illustrate issues kids would most likely be dealing with: depression, divorce, friendship, alcohol. After chapel we broke into small groups for Bible lessons, which were facilitated by counselors who had worked at camp in previous years. After the small groups we ate lunch and then had a short break.

While I tried to spend time with the other counselors, I had a hard time connecting with anyone, aside from my beginning conversations with May and Jill. And even though I felt isolated, almost everyone greeted me with a hug, just like Catherine on the first day. Hugs were such a common greeting that I learned the particulars of each person's. Cheryl's hug, for example, reminded me of touching the inside of a clam. Her skin was warm and damp and her round body made it hard for me to wrap my arms around her back. The hugs kept me connected to these people in a small but real way.

We ended every day of counselor training on the shore. After a week of being at camp I looked over the crowd of people who had made the decision I did, kids from small liberal arts colleges, with summer tans and frayed jean shorts, wearing handmade crosses constructed from colorful plastic beads or from twigs held together with knots of dried grass. The church kids. The rebel kids. After only a week, everyone was seduced by the energy of the place and the possibility that miracles might exist.

I too wore a cross, one carved from driftwood by a tall, dark boy. Though we barely spoke, he pulled me into a building one afternoon to present me with his gift, telling me he thought I could use a smile. Camp was made up of those moments where people randomly pulled you aside to pray for you, bless you, tell you they had premonitions about your future, or adorn you with a carved cross. These moments of recognition became addicting, filled with the power of unsolicited attention and, more importantly, messages from God.

At the shore we settled onto large logs that formed a circle around the fire pit. The breeze from the lake was steady, ruffling our hair and carrying the nutty scent of smoke. Two boys with white teeth and sandy hair pulled into ponytails played guitar. While the guitars filled the night air with music, the waves kept a beat. When the singing began, it felt like the Holy Spirit had literally come to join us on the lake. Jesus's words came into my mind while I sat on my log. "When two or more are gathered in my name, I am there." Almost every night tears streamed down my cheeks. Hidden sniffles from the crowd told me that I was not alone in my unnamed sadness.

After the singing came "sharing." Sharing, I learned, was where we each stood in front of the group, one at a time, to share where we were in our journey with God. Every night about three people stood—moved, we collectively believed, by the power of the Holy Spirit, when it was their chosen time.

Unfortunately, after a week around the fire, the Holy Spirit was not moving me to make a personal confession in front of strangers. My own spirit was telling me to flee, telling me I'd rather stand naked in front of these people than share my personal journey. Clearly, if I was to talk about where I was with God, I would need to tell them I was gay—I now thought—which I was barely prepared to do with my close friends. Admitting I was trying to decide how I should even think about God, in light of what I had learned at school, seemed like a terribly inappropriate topic too, since I was days from being an official camp counselor who was supposed to influence vulnerable little kids.

I listened carefully to each person who stepped out of the silence to stand in front of the fire and confront the glowing eyeballs of the crowd. Each of the stories had a protagonist: a bad relationship, alcohol, drugs, or pain from a challenging parent. I was certain there were other ways people had fallen out of grace with God, but there was an unspoken agreement that some sins wouldn't be named, like sex. Presumably, we were all virgins.

Several of the women gushed with emotion, sobbing. It is almost as if they had been waiting for this moment of confession their entire lives. As they released their words, guilt slid off their souls like the skin from a boiled potato, exposing the white holiness of their new beings.

Most of the young men stood with their hands in their pockets, kicking the earth and circling the fire with their eyes on the ground. They talked in low voices about how they had been "too proud" or jerks, but now wanted to return to God.

There were a few, the innocent church kids like Cheryl, who had yet to experience the tragedy of being separated from God. Instead the church kids took the opportunity to practice being missionaries, telling us what amazing things God had done in their lives. "I've heard so many stories of pain and despair. I can tell all of you that you are not alone! God loves you! God is here for you! God will save you! I praise God for the work he has done in my life." So the story went.

Every night the pressure to share grew. I sat on a log, my stomach tightened like that of a six-year-old waiting to receive a dreaded shot. I knew my turn was inevitable. I prayed for the Holy Spirit to find me, to give me a story to tell.

Another vocabulary was used at Bible camp, language filled with praise, spirit, evil, and salvation. The physical world became muted as the spiritual world came to life. "I was on my way to chapel and something told me I should go down to the lake. I found Blake there, deeply upset by something. God brought me to him." There was a war at hand, because camp was not just the home of God, it was also, apparently, a place where the Devil lurked, ready to snatch weak souls. "I am sure the Devil is interfering with the Lord's work. The phone rang when we were praying.

That's not coincidence, that's the Devil. He's desperate because he knows God is working here."

We were taught that we must unite in a spiritual warfare to combat this evil force. The prize? Innocent souls, including mine. I quickly assimilated to this way of understanding the world and expressing myself. For the next few months, I would no longer be able to separate action and consequence from the presence of a spirit.

On the last night of our counselor training I could barely eat my supper. I knew the time had come for me to step into the circle and share my story. After we ate, we all went to our rooms to throw on sweaters and jeans. I pulled my clothes on slowly and rehearsed possible speeches in my head. *What can I tell them about? I cannot talk about my hellish year at college, where my dreams about being with a woman were destroyed.* I was unsure of what I had gotten myself into. This was not going to be a summer of romping through wildflowers in the mountains. All I wanted to do was to go home.

During this time I thought a lot about my family and my small town. We did not talk about spirits at Wyndmere Lutheran Church. There were no evil forces or attacks from the Devil. Mostly there was just our routine. Sunday mornings started with Dad blasting the oldies station on the radio. My siblings and I covered our heads while Dad sang along with the Beach Boys, flipped our lights on and off, and ordered "Everyone up!"

The four of us resisted as long as we could. Finally, when I couldn't take the music any longer, I got up, switched the station to the "Top Forty Countdown" and turned up Wham! or Madonna. When I wasn't looking, Dad switched it back to his station. The entire way to church David and I battled for control of the radio while Dad lectured us on "real" music.

In church Dad smelled like fried food and coffee. I sat near him in the pew, taking long, deep breaths and thinking the peculiar onion and coffee smell was simply the scent of his suit coat. I thought this was Dad's unique church smell until I sat with Jessica's family one morning and realized that her dad had a suspiciously similar suit coat smell. It dawned on me then that I was inhaling the secondhand scent of the Main Street Café. Before church the farm men, including my dad, had coffee and talked about the crops while the kids went to Sunday school classes the women taught.

Before I came along, Mom was Catholic and Dad was Methodist. Mom seemed to care more about church than Dad. Even so, Dad refused to go to a Catholic church except on Christmas (back then small-town denomination rivalry was as strong as school rivalry), so Mom gave in and we became Methodist. Then, after Antelope no longer drew enough families with kids to keep Sunday school going, Mom and Dad compromised and we started to go to the Lutheran church in town.

I wasn't happy with the decision. In a small town you identify everyone by a name, a job, and a religion. Choosing a denomination seemed like a big decision. I wanted a connection to something larger. I wanted to be able to say "my family is Lutheran" and feel like it meant something, like we had generations of Lutherans that had come before us. Instead I sort of felt like I was borrowing a religion that really wasn't mine.

On occasion Mom took us with her to the Catholic church. That kind of church made sense to me. There was emotion and drama as soon as you pushed through the door. A bronze statue of Jesus nailed to the cross hung on the wall. The creases in his brow showed the nearness of death. Stained glass twisted light into color before it entered the holy space. Incense filled the air. Kneeling, I contemplated my sins and how lucky I was that Jesus died for me. The Catholic church was mysterious and holy, grand and delicate at the same time.

Wyndmere Lutheran Church had a steeple and sat across the street from the school. The altar was small, decorated with only a wooden cross, which was illuminated by a neon light that seemed better suited for a gas station. Purple felt banners with hand-glued letters hung on the walls. I knew that I was supposed to view my white Lutheran church as God's house, but it seemed to me that if this was true, God would have made much more interesting decisions about the decor.

When Jessica and I started wearing our Jesus T-shirts, I became very critical of the church. On Sunday mornings my teachers filled the church pews. These were the last people I wanted to see on my day off. And, even worse, kids from school slipped into the pews with their parents. I knew these people weren't concerned with being good or with God.

My sharing time had come. Unable to put it off any longer, I walked slowly down to the beach. I had the same feeling I still do in dreams where I am heading to math class but have not done my homework all semester. The night was especially dark, with little light from the moon. I smelled the infant fire and knew the boys were stoking it.

The sidewalk to the lake ended at soft sand. I stepped onto the sand, walked over to the logs, and sat. I stretched my sweater over my knees and wrapped my arms around my legs. *Maybe I can shrink,* I thought. *Maybe I can melt into the sand, be lost among the millions of small grains.*

Ironically, the thought of missing my turn was even more terrifying than sharing. My instincts told me that if I didn't get up, I would go unnoticed for the rest of the summer. There were, after all, forty counselors, and most of them had stepped into the summer as if they had waited their entire lives to be camp counselors. Like Jill, they were open, gregarious, and ready to embrace their newfound salvation. I was not.

I decided to be the second person to share. I would jump up immediately after the first person, to ensure I was neither the first nor the last. The first person to share was one of the church kids, making the entire presentation boring—an ineffective distraction. I took shallow breaths and waited. As soon as she sat down, I stood and walked into the silence.

The most uncomfortable part about sharing was that nobody was facilitating, nobody was leading. Catherine was in the crowd, somewhere, probably with head bowed, praying for everyone who stepped into the circle. I was slightly light-headed. The fire was crackling. I felt the sand underneath my feet. Most of the faces were lost in the dark night. My light-headedness was replaced by an out-of-body feeling that gave me the space I needed to move into my words.

"God has always been a part of my life," I began, hearing myself, not entirely in control of what I was saying or aware of what might come next. Maybe this was the Holy Spirit talking, I hoped.

"You know, when I was little I always thought that God was with me. I talked to Jesus on a daily basis. I said my prayers. I didn't question. In fact, I'd say that Jesus was my best friend." I paused. Swallow. Hands in pockets. Hands out of pockets.

I continued. "During that time in my life I was aware of how God helped me through hard moments—fights with friends, fights with my parents—moments where I felt alone or afraid. In those situations I would pray for God to help me. He always did."

Then, miraculously, after the first few sentences I started to relax. The people blurred into the dark and my senses opened to the natural world. I heard the waves and smelled the breeze off the lake. It carried a damp, fishy smell.

"I have tried to continue to incorporate God into my life. I have a strong feeling of peace when I am connected to God and a strong feeling of sadness when I am not. When I feel connected, I know that everything happens for a reason." I circled the fire and heard my words feeding the air. Suddenly I was aware of the crowd. I was a performer; they were my audience.

"Over the last few months I have felt a strong force surrounding me. This force is dark, heavy, evil." I heard a few gasps from the land of eyeballs. Though I knew better, I continued.

"This force has made me do things I have not wanted to do, it has pushed me away from God, from goodness." I paused with dramatic intent. "I've always been aware of good and evil, right and wrong." My voice rose to meet the waves, to claim the moment, to tell a story with purpose. "And at this point in my life, it is almost like I am being *attacked*. It is like the *Devil* is coming for me. Like a spiritual war is happening in my heart!" *Liar!* my mind screamed. *What are you doing? Shut up.* Perhaps there was, indeed, a war for my soul, but to myself I had not attributed it to the Devil. Truth was, I was now evoking the language I had learned at camp, simply so I would belong.

After my dramatic admission, when I looked out over the water with a face that probably looked possessed, I returned to my seat on the log. I felt phony, empty, fake. Two counselors near me hovered close, putting their arms around my shoulders and holding me between them. I cried (protocol after sharing). The next person stood up to share. I sat quietly between the two strangers who pressed their bodies to me as if applying an emotional tourniquet. As another voice filled the night air, my stomach ached with regret. My sharing moment was over. I didn't feel relieved. In fact, I felt worse. I was receiving comfort from people for a ridiculous story about being attacked by evil spirits. My face burned with the red stain of embarrassment.

We ended the evening by singing two songs. I swayed with the rest of the crowd, still being held closely. When we finally stood up a tall, gangly boy nicknamed Thorn walked toward me. Thorn had white-blond hair and a ghost-like complexion. Since being at camp I had learned that Thorn was actually the ringleader of the spiritual police. That is, he was the leader of a small pack of people who cast off demons, performed exorcisms, and best understood the mysterious spiritual world surrounding camp.

"Hey, Melanie. Can I talk to you for a minute?" Thorn's voice was soft, positive. My emotional tourniquets handed me to him, knowing that I was in need of his healing powers.

"Sure," I said, not sure what else to say. I followed him to a picnic table near the water. A few people walked on the beach in the distance. Most made their way back to the camp.

"You were really brave to share your story tonight." I felt queasy, like I did when talking to the campus pastor. "I wanted to ask you a little bit about this spiritual force that seems to be attacking you. How long has it been going on?" I had been successful. I had warranted an intervention from the spiritual police.

"Well, I've always been very aware of the spiritual world around me." I said. This was actually true. When I was little I was fascinated with scary stories and convinced that I was not alone. Sometimes at night I would crawl into the foot of my parents' bed, unable to shake my feelings.

"Recently, I've felt a similar awareness." This was not so true. Until this moment, I had not blamed the Devil for my confusion or my hard year. Thorn stared at me with intent, serious eyes. He sat quietly. I figured I'd better keep talking, but I was not sure what to say. The pause ended when Thorn took my hand.

"There are many evil forces at work, especially here at camp where we are trying to do God's work. The Devil is really quite serious." I looked at him, wondering if he was being empathetic, or if he was warning me about playing with such topics. "If you don't mind, I'd like to say a prayer for you." I nodded my head.

We both bowed our heads. There is a strange energy that exists when praying with another person. The first few seconds are strained and full of anxiety, but after the first words are spoken comfort fills the space.

"Lord, I pray for your child Melanie tonight. I ask that you come into her heart, fill all of the lonely spaces. Protect her from evil forces." He paused. I am not sure if he expected me to say anything, but I could not physically bring myself to participate. "Lord, I ask that you guide her to make the right choices." *Choices.* The word struck me as odd. Evil spirits were attacking me, where do my choices fit into this? "Fill her with your love.

Release her from worry. Guide her this summer. In your name
we pray. Amen." To my great relief, we were finished.

Thorn looked at me after our prayer. I could tell he felt good,
powerful. I, on the other hand, felt stupid and embarrassed.

"Thank you." I didn't know what else to say.

"Don't thank me, thank God," he said and I felt corrected
again. We both got up and started walking back to camp.

God's Followers

When the first batch of campers arrived I was assigned to kitchen duty. I was convinced my assignment had something to do with my sharing confession, as if I need to be monitored for evil spirits before I could come into contact with the kids. Cheryl was in the kitchen too, which brought a hopeless comfort to my situation. She was easy and required little effort. But she was also one of the church kids, which meant my week would be happy and likely boring.

I spent my days chopping vegetables and preparing food for armies of little spiritual warriors. I stared into large vats of gravy and watched from behind the long serving counter while the other counselors delighted in the hero worship from the gaggle of junior high kids who followed them into the dining hall. Cheryl swung large wooden spoons filled with mashed potatoes in the air while she danced around the kitchen and praised the Lord. She rallied me and the other counselors to join her in a chant: "Kitchen crew! Kitchen crew!"

After everyone ate we always got a routine cheer from the kids, led by Catherine. "Let's give a holler for our kitchen crew!" Cheryl went crazy at this, waving her wooden spoon even higher. Embarrassed, I mustered a fake smile and avoided the eyes of May and Jill, who sat among their kids.

I didn't get a group of kids my second week of camp either. Instead I was assigned to an off-site day camp in a small Iowa town. At day camp, we stayed with volunteer families for the week. I didn't know what to expect as I rode in a large van with five other counselors who had the same assignment. We had a map, a schedule, our Bibles, and small packs of clothes. The map led us down gravel roads to farmhouses where we were let out, one by one, to meet each of our assigned families who would feed and shelter us for the week.

When it came to my stop we pulled into a long driveway. At the end of the driveway was a large, old farmhouse surrounded by green pastures. When I got out of the van I could hear a creek in the distance.

I was put at ease when an old couple named Florence and Brownie met me at the door. Florence showed me to my room, which had one window that overlooked a pasture of horses and another that overlooked winding gravel roads. Unlike in North Dakota, where the gravel is yellow, the Iowa gravel roads were white, creating great contrast to the blue skies and green earth. I was, for the first time since arriving at camp, at home.

Every morning the camp van pulled into the yard at seven thirty and gave a polite honk. I joined the other counselors for a day of crafts and singing with second-graders. In the afternoon the van dropped me back at the farm where I took walks. When I returned from my walks I sat in the kitchen with Florence, helping her make supper.

Food was a high priority at this farm. Florence and Brownie were both portly and beamed with delight when we sat around their table. In the mornings Florence served baskets of home-made muffins with butter and jam. For supper she served steam-ing dishes of potatoes and yams, covered with golden brown cheese, alongside chicken and beef. Brownie always delighted in telling me, right before my first bite, the origin of my supper. "That right there, young lady, is old Jerry's cow. Got a whole side of beef this spring. Darn good, huh? That Jerry." He paused to wipe his mouth and shake his head as if he could barely believe his luck, knowing Jerry and all. "Best beef in Iowa." This was months before I became a vegetarian.

The farmhouse was old, creaking, loaded with character, and incredibly large for just the two of them. The floors were made of wide cedar and secured with hundred-year-old nails. Large woven rugs warmed up each room. Old tools hung from hooks on the walls, not as decor but as things Brownie grabbed on his way to mend a fence or expel a stubborn root.

I liked Florence. Her eyes were warm and wise. They reflected a youthfulness that had already expired in the rest of her body. Despite just getting off cooking duty at camp, I even enjoyed helping her with supper.

"That man is just going to kill himself. I tell him every year he needs to slow down," she said one afternoon as she made bread and I worked beside her, peeling hard-boiled eggs. "We're not young any more, you know. He just don't seem to understand that he cannot do the same things he could do when he was nineteen." She shook her head and looked up at me. "Plain stubborn."

I was moved by her care for Brownie, her need to talk about him, repeat his name, and criticize him to show her affection. I watched her hands, old and strong, with large knuckles, and knew that she—like Brownie—would work hard until the day she died.

"Foolish," she continued, not yet finished. "You just make sure you get yourself a boy with some good sense." I focused on my egg, carefully peeling the shell, using the nail of my thumb to break the thin skin that encased its slippery meat.

I forced myself to look into Florence's blue eyes and smile. "I will," I said, softly. There was never another good answer.

"Well," Florence continued. Her voice had lost her ranting tone. It sounded calmer, more intentional. "Well," she repeated. "No matter. You don't worry too much about that *boy* nonsense. God always has a plan."

A few weeks after I left Florence and Brownie's farm I sat with a group of families in a cabin by the lake. It was family camp week. The day was in transition, an evening thunderstorm coming up. As the weather turned, we made ourselves cozy on big couches. One of the dads played guitar as the rest of us sang.

When the storm struck, the music died down and conversation began. The topic, as it often was: salvation.

"It is so good to come back here every year, to reconnect with God," the guitar player said, putting his legs up on a chair and resting his chin on the neck of his instrument. "There are very few places these days where you can be surrounded by others who have been saved. The world is an ugly, ugly place."

"We are lucky, so, so lucky, to enjoy this beauty. To have each other. To do God's work. To be chosen," said his wife. I noticed that when people started to talk about God, they felt it necessary to pause in interesting places, like a preacher would, as if the Holy Spirit was speaking through them.

Chosen. The word echoed in the cabin. Am I chosen? There were moments, distinct moments, where I marveled at the tone of my own thoughts, where the simple fact that I could cast a word into my mind to bounce around and vibrate, seemed like a miracle.

Others lingered on this word also. "We are *chosen*, you know," another man jumped in. "There are only so many places in heaven and they are reserved for us. Do you realize this?" Here the man flipped through his Bible and recited a verse to support his claim. "We are lucky, my friends. God has selected us. Though we have free will, we have recognized the Lord in our lives."

I sank into the couch, listening with discomfort. These people assumed that I was chosen too. They showered me with warmth and took me into their families like one of their own children—so thankful for my devotion. I obsessed over my secret, the knowledge that I was different than them. In their eyes life was a gigantic switchboard with duel levers for every situation. You could pull the right lever or the wrong lever. Everything had a correct answer.

I knew that my feelings—and now my experiences with women—propelled me into the category of unredeemable sinner. Kids who were not virgins could claim a second virginity. Kids who did drugs could come clean. All of these minor sins were understandable. In fact, these life challenges gave camp a reason for existing—to help kids work through their sins and become right with God. These kids would never be pushed away from the community.

Though all sins were supposed to have equal weight, and we were all supposed to be sinners seeking God's grace, being gay was different. Being gay was not something you could work on. Gay people didn't come to camp. They were part of the rest of the world, the *ugly* world, the world that symbolized the reason for the inevitable second coming of Christ.

During this same week, I had been on another tour of kitchen duty with one of the church kids I didn't know well. She wasn't happy and light, like Cheryl. Instead she was distant, perfectly put together, at camp for the summer before graduating from college and marrying her longtime boyfriend.

On our first meal together I threw on my apron and prepared to cut carrots and potatoes for the evening meal of roast beef.

"Did you go to the visiting speaker?" I asked, forcing conversation with a person who was as uninterested in me as I was in her. We shared the love of Christ and that was about it. My question ignited her, as if she had been granted permission to get something off of her chest.

"Oh, it was excellent. Just excellent." I watched her cut the potatoes carefully in half. Another precise slice and they were in quarters. Next she placed them into a kettle filled with water, which was sitting on the cutting table between us. She was a perfectionist.

"What did he talk about?" I offered, an obligatory prod.

"He talked about the danger we are facing in the world right now. You know—the increase in crime, rape, murder, and homosexuality."

Deep breath, concentrate on the potato.

"Interesting," I said, chopping my potatoes in uneven chunks. "Did he equate homosexuality with murder and rape? They seem to be on fairly different levels when it comes to sin." I scratched her itch. She picked up her pace on the potatoes.

"They're on *exactly* the same level. They are all horrendous sins and, as he was saying, are changing the makeup of society as we know it."

"Huh," I said, trying to focus and act unmoved. "What if one of your campers confided in you about her feelings for another girl?"

"Kids just don't have those feelings. Homosexuality is a perverted sin and obviously something that has been planted in their heads. That is *exactly* the problem with this world. These kids are getting bombarded with messages. Homosexuals go to their schools to recruit them." This, of course, confused me. I didn't know any lesbians when I was growing up in North Dakota. On what planet did recruiting happen?

"Huh," I said again, not wanting to agree and not wanting to incriminate myself either. We ended there.

As I listened to the conversation of the "chosen" families on that rainy night and thought of my recent encounter in the kitchen, I grew more and more uncomfortable with camp and my inclusion in this elite club of people selected for salvation. I became dizzy with anger. I knew I was "chosen" by the simple fact that I could cast a word into my head, hear my voice and think. I wasn't going to be recruiting little kids to be gay. What in the hell did that mean? Yes, I was chosen but, I believed, so was the rest of humanity. If not, why were we all here?

I looked at Florence flipping chicken on the cutting board. Her kind demeanor was textured with wisdom and freedom. I envisioned her talking to God when I was not there, criticizing Brownie to the Great Force she believed brought her simple goodness each day.

Though there was no physical resemblance, Florence reminded me of my mom: humble, playful, unassuming, and loving.

I suspected that if Florence and Brownie believed there were only so many tickets to heaven, they would have given up their seats for others, unable to live with others' suffering. And I suspect that as Florence watched me peeling an egg, as if peeling the invisible layers of my shame, she meant exactly what she said: God always has a plan.

We sat down to have breakfast on the morning I had to leave. Brownie was wearing his suspenders and Florence was still in her pajamas.

"This has just been a pleasure, my dear," Florence said to me, as I bit into my last homemade muffin. "A true pleasure."

"For me too. I appreciate this so much." I meant this. I would have traded the rest of my time at camp to be able to stay with Florence and Brownie.

"You hold a special place with us, you know. This will be our last year of taking in counselors. Brownie needs to rest and I'm just getting old."

"Ridiculous," I said, just like I had been saying all week when she brought up how old they were.

"Well, truth is I am losing my eyesight and don't know how much longer I'll be able to get around by myself." Even though she was saying the words, plain as day, I didn't understand. "And Brownie, old goat, he's got liver cancer and isn't doing the best."

"What?" I asked, perplexed.

Sadness landed on Florence's face, like a mask meant for someone else.

None of this had come up earlier in the time I'd spent with them. Visions of the beautiful farm and the old farmhouse rushed through my head. All of this seemed so precious and temporary, as if time now meant something. I was aware of my youth.

"Now, don't you go away worrying." Florence saw the panic on my face. "Don't you think another thought about us, you silly girl. This is the cycle of life. This is all a part of our journey and we're gonna be just fine."

I thought of those at camp who harnessed the miracles of God, who claimed to have the power to heal and transform. Their desire to fight fate suddenly stuck me as a self-righteous inclination.

I knew Florence believed her words. "We're gonna be just fine." And so I felt a strange peace about the news. Just then, the van honked in the driveway.

"Thank you," I said, looking into Florence's blue eyes that now held new meaning, and gave her a hug. "Thank you for everything."

May was the only person I confided in that summer. We were in the laundry room washing our clothes on a rainy night. I was sitting on the dryer she was on the floor folding laundry. The washer and dryer were warm on the chilly night. We could have been a pair of cats, curled next to the heat.

I had come to know May well enough, though I kept a comfortable emotional distance from her and the few I considered friends. My intuition on this night told me to trust her, to let go of my secret, to test the waters. I was, after all, leaving soon. Why would it matter if she rejected me?

"So, I had a relationship with a woman at school," I finally said, after we had changed several loads and hours had gone by. She didn't flinch. Her eyes were peaceful, curious. She maintained the same softness she'd had when she sat by me on that first night. I told her, then, about growing up, about Jessica, about the wolves. I shared with this one girl all of the stories that did not make their way to the fire pit during my "sharing" confession.

I have learned that in most cases, when I am brave enough, when I speak the words that make me uncomfortable to the point of nausea, my truth makes room for an opening within the other person. They return, almost without question, my honesty. Their stories flow from them with the same vulnerability I presented to them. Though it is so easy to forget, I am rarely the only one with a secret.

My confession opened May. She too had a story, one about sex, confusion, and pain. She talked about him then, running her hands through her hair, her face getting flushed. It was a complicated situation, she told me, hard to explain. I listened, as she had listened to me. I tried to understand why she was tiptoeing, why I had not heard about her boyfriend this entire summer, when we were in a world where people wore their "back home" relationships like a watch.

She told me about giving her first blow job, making love, and about how she had been sneaking around, but now had to stop—had to end the relationship. I thought I understood her dilemma. It was, after all, a sin to have sex outside of marriage. Blow jobs were probably worse. But still, she could be forgiven. She could take on a second virginity, as many people did, I was told.

At the end of the evening, before May went off with her clean laundry, she was quiet for a time, considering, it seems, whether or not she could really trust me. As if her secret was somehow more incriminating than mine, which couldn't possibly be true. Then she spoke again: "I've been having sex with my stepbrother," she said. "It just happened," she added. Then she picked up her last load and left.

The Plainness of Holiness

I am about midway through my harvest retreat. Today Mom is going to give me a brushup on how to drive the tractor. For the last several days she has been out in the field, following the progression of harvest, pulling the chiseler over the recently combined land.

When we get out of our cars (I drove separately, in case I don't want to be in a tractor all day) I look around and notice a few buildings across the road. One of them, the largest, is hidden behind a grove of trees, barely visible. "Mom, let's check that out first," I say and direct her attention to my find.

We walk across the road. Two small buildings and a parked truck sit out in the open. We study them for a minute and then trudge through the trees to a larger building.

"Looks like someone converted an old building into some sort of grain storage shed," I say, trying to decipher what we're looking at. The building is covered in corrugated steel, making it resemble a square grain bin or a Valentine's Day box wrapped in aluminum foil.

"Wait. Is it a—church?" Mom asks. "Mel, yes! Look at the windows. It used to be a church."

Wood paneling covers what appears to be the familiar shape of arched stained-glass windows. The rest of the building's identity suddenly pops with this context. "Sure enough. Look at the steeple on top." I point to the top of the building. "A church converted to a grain bin?" I ask, still not sure.

I remove a bolt holding the front doors shut. "Should we go in?" I ask, a bit leery of what might be inside.

"Sure," Mom says.

"What if rats run out?" I say, losing my nerve.

Mom looks at me and shrugs. "I'm sure it will be fine."

"Easy for you to say. I'm first," I respond. Then, before thinking any more about it, I pull my arms to my chest—in the event I have to deflect flying rats—and kick the doors open.

Fortunately, the doors creak open without incident. Mom and I step into what looks like a church entrance, further confirming our suspicion. "It's dark in here," I say.

"Look there," Mom says, pointing to a stairway. "That must have led to the balcony."

I happen to be carrying Mom's camera in my pocket because I wanted to take pictures in the field. I start snapping pictures to afford us some light.

All of the walls are boarded up with plywood. In front of us is what used to be a small sanctuary. At first there seems little left to indicate that this was once a place of worship—no pews, no pulpit, no hymnals. The building is empty aside from seed bags and a couple of shovels. Then, after a few more flashes, I notice something.

"Mom, are those words above the altar?" I am whispering for no good reason. Large letters appear to be scribbled on an arch above where an altar used to be.

"I can't see. What do they say?" she whispers back.

"I can't tell." I snap a few more times, but the light doesn't last long enough for us to make sense of the illuminated words.

After a few more minutes of investigation we leave the church, replace the bolt, and make our way back to the field. As we walk I bring the pictures up on the camera screen. I find a picture of the arch and zoom in on the elaborate, gothic lettering.

"Mom, the words say 'That Is Slain Is Worthy.'"

"What?" Mom asks.

"That Is Slain Is Worthy," I repeat. "I'm sure they probably meant that *which* is slain is worthy but didn't have enough room to fit it all. You know, like the lamb who was slain?" I say, remembering my Bible lessons. "Freaky—if you ask me."

"Huh." Mom responds.

I can't help but imagine an old-time prairie cult whose parishioners made human or animal sacrifices at the altar to prove their worth.

"You've never noticed this building before?" I ask.

"No." Mom shakes her head.

Mom and I continue to the field, where we resume my tractor lesson. I watch her procedure for a couple of rounds—raise and lower the chisel, work around wet spots, turn at the headlands—then I take over. Driving the machine comes back to me easily. I take hold of the wheel, nudge the lever to accelerate, hit a button to lower the equipment behind us, and head to the other end of the field. The ride is rough, slow, and jerky. It feels like we are on horseback, pulling logs through a muddy stream. After I am up to speed we bounce together for hours, talking and laughing while transforming the land as easily as dragging a decorating comb over a frosted cake.

For the next couple of days the fragmented message in the grain-bin church irritates me like a tiny sliver. Walking around the farm, I repeat the message like a riddle: *That is slain is worthy. That is slain is worthy.* I envision children in the pews, wearing pioneer clothing, looking down at their shoes, ingesting unworthiness, and embarking upon lifetimes where they—sinners to the bone—seek redemption like hungry animals.

I think of myself as a child and the journey I've taken since.

It seems a lifetime since I left Bible camp. On that late summer day—my last day at camp—I opened the windows of my packed car as I drove away. The lake breeze was warm against my face. I turned up the radio and sang at the top of my lungs. I had never felt freedom like that in my life. I did not realize until that very moment that I had not really been breathing all summer. Not, at least, the kind of breathing where your whole body relaxes and your organs get drunk on oxygen.

After that summer I was stunted for a time, my spiritual growth arrested. The God I talked to as a child, the God my mom relied on to soothe my pains, the God Jessica and I had championed as teenagers was not *my* God, but the God of the people I met at camp. And those people introduced me to judgments about the world I couldn't accept. The most painful judgment was about the way I would love another person. My idea about love had always seemed to me as natural as the crops. After I left camp I knew that some thought my love was darkened by sin.

My gradual estrangement from the structured church was not immediate, but long, lingering, and thoughtful. I now marvel at the human soul's ability to recognize injustice, immorality, and corruption, even when those traits are hidden within the most confusing oxymoron imaginable: power-hungry, mind-controlling, corporation-like entities shrouded in the façade of divinity. Not all churches or religious institutions should be described this way, but if you dare deconstruct the story, dare pull at the dangling threads of the human institutions, oftentimes—as numerous scholars, writers, and seekers have discovered and articulated better than I can here—the truths that unravel can be hard to accept.

At age nineteen I knew—though everything around me told me otherwise—that something was not quite right at camp. Something was not aligned with the God I felt. And I had to learn to trust my voice, despite the condemnation that comes with questioning the façade.

Along the way since I have explored other religions, other ways of explaining existence, and other methods of connecting to something divine. And these explorations have fortunately allowed me to retain a reverence for mystery. And my reverence for mystery has allowed me to retain a connection to something good, something *there*.

—∞—

Over the years I have started to see the holy in surprising places. When I study my dad, for example, I witness his life as a holy practice. Each year he opens the earth, inserts life, takes the gifts, and moves quietly into winter. His commitment, practice, and routine rival those of the most devout yogi, meditation practitioner, or priest. To share this observation with him, however, would certainly elicit a deep furrow of his brow. He would think the city has made me crazy.

I witness a sense of holiness in my mom too, the woman who introduced me to God, the person who taught me my first prayers and told me we pay for the sins of others.

"Pay for the sins of others? Hmmm. Well, I might of thought that at one time, but I certainly don't think that today," she'll tell me later. "In fact, that's stupid. Don't go telling people I said that," she'll continue, rolling her eyes self-consciously.

She'll give me books about past lives or near-death experiences, along with books on Mother Teresa. When I complain about religion, about the gender inequality of the Catholic Church, for example, she'll say, "I know, but nothing's perfect, dear." Her ability to cling to pieces of convention while exploring a wide range of possibilities for our existence is where I see the beauty of her holiness—she is infinitely more open-minded than me.

Recently Mom gave me a book on hell. "Here," she said. "You should read this. See what hell is all about."

"Mom, I'm not sure I even believe in hell. Why are you reading this stuff?" I turned the book around. Printed on the cover, on which flames were depicted, was the claim that the author had spent time in hell. "Honestly, this is probably a book meant to scare the crap out of you so you'll do whatever this dude suggests."

"Well, I've read books about people who have gone to heaven. Thought I'd better read about hell too." She sat for a moment. I thought she was considering my input about brain-washing, but instead she said, "You better read it. Hell is *not* a place you want to go."

"Mom. Who goes to hell? Think of how many people in the world are not born into Christianity." I used the common, obvious argument that "one way" may have a few kinks. "And what about the millions of souls who roamed this earth before Christianity was even conceived?"

"Well—yes, those people can hardly help it, honey. I know what you are saying. All *I* am saying is that if there *is* a hell, why not believe what you are supposed to and avoid it? That way you are safe."

"You are not understanding me," I said, frustrated.

"I understand where you are coming from, but all I am saying is read the book. You will want to avoid hell, I'll tell you that much."

With this I couldn't avoid a spontaneous outcry: "Oh, Mom."

We've had this same back and forth about church. A couple of years ago I was home when Mom and Dad still lived on the farm, and Mom came to wake me. "Honey, you should go to church." She was dressed and ready for Sunday morning Mass.

"*Mom,*" I said, not wanting to hear a lecture.

"Don't you miss the fellowship and community?" she said with a stern face.

"Mom, *fellowship*? Seriously?" Even in my morning grogginess, I couldn't help but let out a laugh. *Fellowship* is not a word Mom uses, but I suspect she figured it fit the subject.

"Yes, fellowship. Don't get smart with me," she said, backing up and holding two earrings to her ears so I could tell her which one to wear. "Which one looks better?"

"The one on the right."

"I know there are probably things you don't *agree* with, but don't you believe in *God*?"

"Yes, I do, Mom. In some way, I guess. But—I'm just not really into church any more. Church isn't the only place I can connect with God. Don't *worry* about me."

"Isn't there a church by you? There must be dozens. Aren't you missing out? Church is where I see all of my friends. Church is where I get my *fellowship*! I'd think that if you found a nice church, it would be a great place to meet friends."

I rolled over and propped myself up on a pillow. "Mom, look, to live here and not go to church would probably be a major void because the entire town goes. I get it. But I don't live here. And I probably wouldn't know anybody at church in the city anyway."

"Well, that's my point. You'd meet nice friends. I think you are missing out." She fluffed her hair in the mirror. "We're having cookies and coffee after church today. So there." She turned and walked out of the bedroom, and I fell onto my pillow.

Despite my disagreements with Mom, her openness, growth, and ongoing commitment to the church, regardless of what other ideas she is investigating, reminds me that the holy reveals itself to us in new ways as we grow and change. We can collect new perspective and wisdom, while not totally dismissing our early belief systems.

Ryan and Montana, who have no time for "religious nonsense," as they'd say, have shown me another kind of holiness. They are vehemently antireligious. For me to even speak about their *hearts* with a straight face would smack of spirituality and would—at least with Ryan—result in the feigned placement of a cold compress to my forehead.

Over hundreds of dinners and traveling through Europe together, through time apart and reunions catching up, over laughs and occasional disagreements, watching ourselves gradually age, I have grown to know the intentions of these two well. I know that while dramatic and judgmental for humorous impact, they are compassionate and caring, good-natured and thoughtful. For me, Ryan and Montana give form to a sort of holiness by demonstrating strong morality not guided by a religious structure. And to do the right thing when nobody is looking is always the noblest act.

When I think of holiness I also think of my grandparents, my mom's parents, devout Catholics. They go to church every Sunday. At their house we say grace at most meals. They have crosses on their walls, holy oil in their bedroom, rosaries at their bedside, and statues of Jesus and Mary in the bedroom where I sleep when visiting. They each take an hour a week to pray as part of their church's twenty-four-hour prayer chain. In my mind's eye I can't separate my idea of them from God and church.

Within their devotion there is something else too, a lightness. As a child I didn't have words to convey the warmth, playfulness, and love I sensed in my grandparents, so I told my mom they were like marshmallow people—"Yes, they are like clouds, like big fluffy puffs, like deep, soft, endless sources of joy."

When I have joined my grandparents at church, I've watched them close their eyes and pray. At the end of the service I have also witnessed their reverence. "Good morning, Father," they'll say, with profound respect, to the man draped in white, waiting to shake our hands, a man I secretly spoke to during the service, begging, through ESP or the Holy Spirit, I'm not sure which, to not mention anything about "the gays," or gay marriage, or hating the sin, while loving the sinner. *Just skip it for today*, I've tried to communicate to him. *God really doesn't care about the gays, with starving people, war, and all.*

I have wondered what they think about their oldest granddaughter not being married, or—even worse—what they think about their granddaughter being a sinner in the eyes of the church. I wondered, that is, until my grandma planted a message in my ear several summers ago, a moment as startling as when an albino squirrel stopped to place a nut in my yard one early morning.

"I read your story," Grandma whispered in my ear. She and I were decorating for a family gathering, putting candles on the table, folding napkins. People around us were laughing, chatting. I was busy arranging silverware. My heart felt as though it had been dropped into a cold pail of water. I knew what she meant. I had published a story where I wrote openly about being gay.

"Really, Gram?" *What! She read my story? Where did she get it? Does Mom have it? Did Mom give it to her? Never mind. What to say, what to say?* "Ah, did you like it?" I whispered back. This was the only response I could think of, framing my question as if I had repainted my room and wanted her opinion.

"Your story was real good. You are a good writer." She paused for a second, and with her aged hand still resting on my shoulder, she continued. "You know, Grandpa and I don't care. It doesn't matter to us. We accept you no matter what." She and I both knew what she meant by *it*. *It* was the unspoken; *it* was the secret that wasn't a secret; *it* was the void between me and most of the people who knew me before I learned how to crawl.

The moment my grandma stashed her nut of love, one she probably wanted to place for the future, for the long winters in my life when she would no longer be able to speak directly to me, was a moment of profound holiness.

My grandparents remind me that the human spirit does have the ability to discern and navigate and love, despite the powerful conditioning of doctrine and politics and institution. It is up to all of us to choose.

Before Bible camp I righteously judged the Lutheran church in Wyndmere. I judged the pastor and his repetition. I judged the organ player. I judged the old men wearing their same pressed suits every Sunday. I judged the women with circles of rouge on their cheeks. I judged their quiet. I judged routine. When I finally arrived at Bible camp, where I thought I would finally be with *true* believers, and where I was supposed to find God in chapel, Bible study, late-night conversation, saving souls, daily hugs, and Bible verses, I often thought about the people in my quiet hometown church. I wanted, in those Bible camp days, my hometown's relaxed, casual, God-on-Sunday-only attitude.

I now understand that there were lessons for me in the routine of my small town, where people come together to eat ham sandwiches and celebrate life's small experiences. They were not waving their arms, singing hallelujah, or clapping their hands, but there was a lesson in their loyalty and in their quiet faith. And there probably still is. Maybe the Lutheran church of my childhood, with its distracted characters, demonstrated the sort of faith that makes sense to me as an adult: a faith with room for life, a faith with room for laugher, a faith that allows us to be imperfectly human. Here too is holiness.

There is a memory I access so infrequently, a good part of me wonders if it wasn't a dream. I was home. The earth was blue in the way it can be when winter sets in and casts its light over the tilled black fields. Mom and I had just finished a walk and were resting on the steps of the Homestead Church by the farm, not saying a word. Snow started to fall, the finest sort of snow, as soft as the dust left in the air after a baker coats a pan with flour. We leaned back on the steps, closed our eyes, and let the flakes mist our faces.

While the time frame of this memory is not entirely clear, I know I was in college and had already worked at Bible camp. What happened on that day, though, was completely incongruent with my larger reality at the time.

After sitting on the steps for a bit, I got up and tried the door. When growing up, I had hungrily peered through cracks in the church's edifice. The building was perpetually locked and had frosted windows, making it impossible to see inside. There had been a precious handful of times, however, when a tug at the door made it give way, allowing David and me to tiptoe around the church until, presumably, a caretaker identified the breach and locked it again.

On this day with Mom, the door opened. I hadn't been in the church for years and was thrilled at our good fortune. And, just like years later when we snuck into the grain-bin church, on this afternoon we first glanced around (as if there was a reasonable threat of someone watching) and hurried inside.

The Homestead Church hadn't held a service in my lifetime. Yet, aside from an abundance of dead flies, the sanctuary looked as if it was set for Sunday. Hymnals lined the rails of the wooden pews. The winter light warmed the space as if we had stepped into a snow globe. The altar was set as if a pastor would soon emerge. On the left side of the altar sat a pump organ, with a music book resting on its ledge and a tiny stool at its base.

I sat on the stool, pulled out a few of the levers on the organ and pumped the bellows with my feet. Next I gingerly pushed the keys. There is nothing as haunting, or maybe as sad, as hearing the raw notes of that organ escape into the silent prairie after year of idleness. The same goes for ringing the church bell, which can be done by pulling a thick rope in the entryway. The bell sends a deep *bong* over the fields. What must people think—shuffling in their yards, finishing chores before the snow flies—to hear a church bell in the distance? "No, couldn't be." They'd pause, tilt an ear, and dismiss.

While I played the organ, Mom looked around the church before settling in the front pew. After a few more minutes of tinkering, I got up and sat beside her. In this, my magical memory, my dream, I feel a calm, as if at vespers, as if in a divine moment of grace, and I tell her, without panic, about what happened at school with the two women, with the wolves. Me, the same person who wanted to squirm out of my own skin when I shared my truth. Me, who couldn't speak a word about my life for years. Me, who never once told her about kissing a boy even, confessed my shame, my sadness, my pain. In this incomprehensible moment at the Homestead Church, I put everything I thought ugly about me, the sin I carried like an anchor around my neck, in front of her, on the little prairie altar. Perhaps then, and in my memory of this moment, is the only time I have ever understood Catholic confession.

My mom, in this otherworldly, snow-globe world, put a hand on my back and told me that I was okay, that people do things—we all do things, these things don't *make* us. And for the first time since grappling with God, with sex, with shame, in that abandoned prairie church I felt what had eluded me, even at camp, where God was supposed to be ever-present, casting out spirits—I felt entirely whole, for a minute, healed.

In this memory I envision all of us collectively in our stronger moments, putting a hand on the back of a loved one—those who can't see their own beauty, who can't hear their own spirits—whispering "it is okay," we are all okay. The acceptance we extend to others, even when we cannot accept ourselves, is one of our greatest gifts of holiness.

The message I now carry with me as I meander on the farm holds its own symbolic truth. "That is slain is holy." The message is incomplete. There wasn't enough room for the full story.

In the end, we are all only trying to find our way through the fragments, really. We are all doing the best we can to grapple with the mystery of existence, usually. Our desire for others to see the world the way we see it is our desire for others to be okay. If we all could just extend that part of ourselves, the hand on the back, constantly, without judgment, without a need for others to change, I think we'd be in a different place. But even as I think this, I hold my own anger, my own resentments, my own judgments. This is not easy.

As I stand on the North Dakota prairie, mumbling to myself about being slain and worthy, I stop and allow the silent land to bring me back to my self, my presence. A fullness wells up in me when I am in this rural world. This is a fullness with perspective, where the wind, and the trees, and sometimes even the faint call of the ocean lead me into a silent mediation. From this space I can imagine a world where we all believe each other worthy. But this image evaporates like the brief sound of a church bell ringing in the distance. *Is it real? No, couldn't be. Or could it?*

Grain Truck Apprenticeship

Today I am up early. I heard Dad stirring before five. We rode to the farm in silence. Now the sun is rising, spreading orange and pink light across the land. I measure the sun by the relative size of the shelterbelts and telephone poles that are toothpick-like silhouettes in the sun's wake-like flood of light. I am sipping Folgers, which is growing on me. When we got to the shop I put an extra scoop in the coffee filter for added jolt.

While the coffee warms and wakes me, I listen to AM radio—Joel's station—and read the *Fargo Forum*. The shop kitchenette is covered in knotty pine, and has east-facing windows looking out over the land. *I'm living the life of a farmer!* I think proudly. (Never mind that the real farmers are outside working. Details, details.) I set up my computer for a morning of writing, thrilled to not be on conference calls and instead watching evidence of the earth's rotation.

In the *Fargo Forum* I notice the headline "Agritourism: A Growing Industry in North Dakota" and read on. "The state Tourism Division wants more North Dakotans to get involved in agritourism, an industry it says is in big demand right now," the article says. It goes on to explain that there is a need for these tours because "more people are interested in knowing where their food comes from as the population becomes more urban." The department will offer workshops for interested farmers, giving them the tools they need to get started in "agritourism."

I put down the paper and look out again at the sunrise. It is as dramatic—as poignant—as any birth, I think. And unlike in the city where, at best, I'll see the final push of the sun over the trees, here the flat land is like an unobstructed birth canal.

Farm tours, hmmmm. I imagine tour buses pulling into the yard and people, cameras dangling from their necks, pushing for the best view. A tour guide would speak into a microphone, "Slow down, folks, there's plenty of room for everyone."

With *oohs* and *ahs* my imaginary tourists step out, stretch, and marvel at the sunrise most of them never see. After the earth's rotation thrusts the sun above the land, the tourists would turn their attention to the grain bins, to the barn, to the fields surrounding them in all directions. What do they do next? Ah, yes: field tours. The tourists would transition to open vehicles. A dozen John Deere Gators would be waiting for them, the farm's mini equivalent of a safari's Land Rover. Donny would give the tourists a quick Gator lesson, just like the kayak guides do before leading trips along the shore of Lake Superior. The lurching Gator caravan would follow my brother to the fields where he would point out various stages of harvest. "And that, my friends, is where your food comes from," he'd say when they all arrived back at the barn with wind-reddened cheeks. (I'd have to coach him to say it that way, but—again—details.)

Even though I grew up here, during the first few years I was away from the farm I realized how little I had absorbed. A friend would quiz me about a just-emerged green crop. I'd mumble for a few seconds, citing something about wheat or pinto beans, but in the end I'd admit that I couldn't tell one short green crop from the next. I hadn't paid attention.

I worked as a child, but my tasks were specific and torturous. Like weeding bean fields where the vines were long and twisted, sticking to my clothes like Velcro. The fields were hot, the sun too strong. The weeds were like small trees, and hard to overcome. I hacked their meaty stems with a machete until white sticky juice, like coconut milk, spilled from the wounds. Each weed removed was a victory, but as I looked across the acres I knew that the weeds had won. As a child I didn't absorb farming details, I avoided them.

One day, years before my harvest retreat, I cornered my dad and asked, "Can you tell me the steps to plant a corn field?" I grabbed my notebook, flipped to a blank sheet, and wrote CORN FIELD on the top of the page. I knew the obvious steps: plow, plant, harvest. But I didn't understand the nuances, the ingredients.

Dad looked at me, humored, I think, by my question. He cleared his throat and began to explain. As he talked I captured the recipe:

CORN FIELD
1. Start with a field, a big flat field.
2. Next, using a tractor and a digger (which is also called a finisher), prepare the land by pulling the digger over the soil with the tractor.
3. Behind the digger, pull a big white tank of anhydrous ammonia. The ammonia dampens the earth with soil-enriching nitrogen.
4. Next, return to the field with a planter. The planter will plug corn seeds into the earth.
5. Over the next several weeks apply 1034-0, a fertilizer.
6. Spray for weeds and bugs. There are several herbicides and pesticides you can use, and they change every year as the weeds and insect pests become immune.
7. Finally, when the corn reaches into the sky, get the combines ready and harvest.

"That it?" I asked.

"Pretty much," Dad said.

I recognized a critical element in this recipe: my family's ability to adapt as farming practices mature, using the appropriate chemicals to keep swarming insects at bay. When I shop in the co-op and reach for organic vegetables, my mind can't help but wander to the land of my childhood, where my family does the best they can to make a living and wouldn't have survived, according to my dad, without chemicals.

"There's no other way," Dad has said. "Look up the statistics. People in cities use almost ten times the amount of chemicals on their lawn per square foot. If you want to blame someone for destroying the environment, it's you city people." He paused, "And those golfers." He ended with a triumphant look on his face. I think he carries these facts because this somehow weighs on his mind.

"Well, I don't use chemicals on my lawn," I have replied.

"Well, maybe that's your problem," he has then said, with a smirk.

"Mornin', Mel. How long you been here?" Donny comes into the shop and pours himself a cup of my extra-strong coffee.

"About an hour."

"Writing?" he asks, seeing the computer open.

"Yes. Doing a little reading first," I say.

"I see," he responds.

"The sunrises are incredible—I'd forgotten."

"Yup, they are," he says, nodding.

"What are you and your little buggy up to this morning?" I have started to refer to the Gator, a small golf-cart-like vehicle, as Donny's "little buggy." He constantly drives it around the farm, like a police officer patrolling an airport on a Segway.

"Oh, well," he says, taking a big breath. "I was out in the field a bit this morning, moving the grain cart. Now I'll probably head over to watch the dryer. Make sure things are going okay. And move some corn, I guess."

By "move some corn," he means from holding tank to leg, from leg to dryer, from dryer to bin. During corn harvest the uninterrupted flow of corn is critical. If any aspect of the complex process breaks down, a code-red panic is evident, as if the grain bins are living entities and the flowing corn is oxygen from ventilators. The corn dryer is the heartbeat of this operation and mostly Dad's domain. Over the years Dad has kept night watch over the dryer. Like a vigilant owl he has monitored the dryer's light from his bedroom mirror. If problems arise the light goes out. When this has happened, Dad has gone out to investigate, sometimes not coming back until dawn.

"So," I say, perking up and smoothing the newspaper in front of me, "I figured out how I can break into the family business."

"Really? Whatcha gonna do?" he smiles.

"Farm tours. I'm gonna be your manager. We're organizing tours for people who want to see where their food comes from. Apparently they'll pay for it!" I point at the paper. "I can quit my job, fix up the barn, and live in it!"

"Oh!" he says. "Think they'll come?"

"No. Not really," I say, "but it's a thing now, farm tours are." He nods, taking my idea completely seriously. "And the North Dakota Tourism Division is holding classes to teach people how to start them. But I don't think I need a class. I've started to map it out—tour buses, Gator rides . . ." Donny listens for a few more minutes while I outline the plan.

During my harvest retreat I stay with Donny and Julia about half of the time, and have determined that my brother is about the most sincere person to walk the earth. I could be predisposed to perpetually seeing my baby brother in a state akin to baby animals—bumbling, sweet, innocent. But this trip is largely about remembering—remembering the land, remembering human connection, remembering my passions, remembering forgotten towns. And so I am also remembering my brother's nature, which is—even accounting for my bias—pleasant, like a sip of whipped-cream-smothered hot cocoa on the grayest of days.

My brother's fate was determined by trial and error, by exploring multiple options. After high school he enrolled in college, but he struggled to determine what he wanted to do with his life. After he decided to leave college he attended a vocational school in Wahpeton to try architectural drafting. I remember admiring his work on a Thanksgiving weekend when my family visited me in Minneapolis. Donny and I sat at a coffee shop, and he worked while I wrote. His sketches were impressive, penciled geometrical lines, beautiful in their representation. However, soon he grew bored and restless with drafting. Through a process of elimination Donny ended up farming—keeping open the possibility the farm might continue in the family after my parents.

What might have been a natural fit, a blessing in disguise— the youngest son returning to the land, keeping a legacy alive— was, at least at first, challenging. Dad never missed a day of work, regardless of how late he had been out the night before. The intensity of Dad's dependability, I have always thought, has something to do with an almost genetically present sense of duty in people who work the land. The early farmers did not answer to a boss. Their loyalty was to the land, to their families. In my dad's case, it was loyalty to his father. The rich land was ready to bless with returns, but not until farmers were willing to give their bodies in a sacrifice. Dad understood this. Dad expected Donny to be working on the farm every morning, of course, no matter how severe the hangover or how great the lack of sleep. But when my brother sleeps, it is as if he has left this world to float high above the clouds. His limbs are heavy, and it is almost impossible to wake him. So when he was not at the farm when the sun rose, Dad drove into Wyndmere to Donny's rented house to retrieve him.

During the early days of Donny's return to the farm, I wondered if my brother might have been one generation removed from the loyalty wired into our grandpa, our dad, and our uncle. Perhaps we all were removed. Our lack of effort never resulted in a loss of basic needs. We always had food, shelter, love, clothes, and toys.

But now Donny is out of the house before I even think about stirring. The days of Dad retrieving his son from slumber are long gone. Donny is here. He is invested. He is a farmer.

When I roam around the farm, escaping my assigned projects, I see little vignettes of Donny going about his day. The images line up like the boxes of a cartoon strip: Donny climbing grain bins, Donny shoveling corn, Donny moving machinery, Donny logging corn moisture numbers by the dryer, Donny buzzing around on his buggy, Donny thrusting his weight at a stubborn, seemingly immovable object. When I ask him details about something related to farming, to his job, he carefully explains whatever I'm asking about like he's addressing the United Nations, involuntary pride settling on his face. I study him, trying to shake the image I have in my mind—toddler, little boy—so I can see him as he is: an adult who has found his way. With this new focus I notice his furrowed brow, strong arms, and rough, unshaven face. I notice the passing of time. I notice the man.

A few days later Donny informs me he will be taking a truck to the field, and says that if I want to I can ride with him. This is my window of opportunity. Donny and Dad never operate the trucks. They stay stationed in the yard, keeping the corn and machinery running. The hired men are usually moving the trucks, and I'm not about to get my truck-driving lesson from a hired man I hardly know.

I should mention: I'm a horribly nervous driver and passenger. Upon returning from trips to Italy and South Africa, I proclaimed myself to be a changed human. My transformation had nothing to do with running into the Indian Ocean, water as warm as tears, or lodging in stone buildings as old as Jesus. No—my transformation occurred as a result of driving in these foreign lands.

Driving in Italy was one thing, with unfamiliar road signs and impatient Italian drivers telling me to get the hell out of the way by flashing lights in my rearview mirror—even on the Amalfi Coast, where the only place to move would have been off the cliff and into the ocean.

But night driving in South Africa was another thing altogether. My traveling companions and I swore we would heed the travel books' advice and not drive after dark—ever. The day I arrived, the locals reported a horrible accident involving a cow, a cart, and a car. Driving on the other side of the road was enough for me. I didn't need to add darkness and cows to the mix. But traveling abroad is unpredictable, so I found myself behind the wheel after dark, swerving in the nick of time, barely avoiding vehicles with no reflectors (short of human eyes) stalled in the right of way.

Throw in the one panic attack I've had in my life—which happened at the end of a solo road trip after college, and during which my heart was beating as quickly as a hummingbird's, and I was certain I was facing untimely death behind the wheel via heart attack—and you have a chronically nervous vehicle occupant.

So when Donny tells me it's time, the first thing that doesn't sit right with me is the actual truck. From what I remember, farm trucks were charming: expanded versions of the Matchbox trucks I pushed around as a kid. But the trucks I remember—the sweet compact blue one and the fire-engine-red one—are parked nearby, windshields cloudy from sitting. I had ignored their idleness until my brother pulls up in a semi.

I can barely pull myself up into the bouncy seat. When I get in, Donny pulls two knobs and the truck hisses like the machine that made Edward Scissorhands. "Why is it making those noises?" I ask.

"These let out the brakes," he says, tapping the knobs he's just pulled. "One for the truck and one for the trailer."

"Okay," I say. Seems reasonable.

When he steps on the gas, the truck lurches like something is caught and dragging behind us. Donny pushes the hissing knobs in again and swings out of the cab like he's parachuting.

After a few minutes I look out and see my brother's hands on the trailer like he's leaning in a urinal, peeing. His head is underneath, studying the tires. Soon Dad joins him. Donny comes back, pushes more buttons.

"What's going on?" I ask.

"For some reason one of the brakes is sticking. We're going to try to release it."

"Release it?"

"Yes. Don't worry, we'll have plenty of other brakes." Donny gives me his big grin, delighting in my panic.

"Should we turn this thing off?" I ask, aware that Dad is somewhere underneath the truck since he's disappeared from my sight.

"Nah," he says and hops down again.

I get out and survey the situation. Dad is lying on his back under the trailer, between wheels—a scene I don't like one bit. Donny is rocking the truck forward and backward with his body. With each thrust the truck moves a few inches. I fear a runaway semi—never mind that the ground is as flat as a skating rink.

"Feels like it's moving," Donny hollers to Dad over the rumble of the truck.

By the time we take off, my irrational driving fear is fully engaged, particularly because Donny tells me we are short a brake ("but no big deal"). I clutch my seat while my brother barrels down the gravel road. I remind myself that he is a grown-up, does this all the time. This is his profession, in fact. "Do you need a special license to drive a semi?" I ask my grown-up, mature, safety-conscious brother.

"Not if you stay so many miles from the farm. I couldn't drive this to Fargo or anything."

"Oh!" I say. "No training, huh? Interesting."

I peek at the speedometer. We are driving sixty-five miles an hour. On gravel. In a semi. When Donny talks I stare straight ahead to model good behavior and encourage him (subliminally) to keep his eyes on the road.

"Scared, Mel?" he asks.

"No," I lie, even though in my head I am screaming at him to put on his seat belt, slow down, and to wrap the entirety of both his God-given hands around the fucking steering wheel. Yes—my fear warrants profanity. Donny is steering with the backs of his hands. In one hand he's holding a Coke; in the other he's holding his phone, flipping through numbers with his thumb.

The turns are the worst. Donny swings wide, to be sure to make the turn, he explains. Because I can't see the road underneath when we swing around, I feel like I'm Thumbelina in the clutches of a giant, being dangled over the ditch. I hold my breath until the semi straightens out again and I can see the road.

"You guys ever tipped one of these things?" The contrived casualness in my voice is ridiculous.

"Not that I know of," he says, calming me a bit until he continues. "Although—Now that I think about it I do remember a time. A hired man tipped a truck at this field, actually. Missed the turn there." He points to a driveway. We turn into the same field at the other end. Donny maneuvers the truck back and forth, like Dad rocking out of the easy chair, before straightening out and driving into the bumpy field. "Tricky turn," he chuckles.

Donny parks the empty truck in the field. I wave at my cousin in the combine. A truck full of corn is ready for Donny and me to take back to the farm. While I've dreamed of truck-driving days with AM radio and grain elevators, I realize that driving truck is a big job. Dad would not be happy to hear that while practicing I dumped a few tons of metal and corn onto the earth.

I make a mental note to e-mail Melissa and explain that if we move back to North Dakota, I will drive a tractor. Driving a tractor is like driving a boat. Is a tractor bouncy, a bit unruly? Sure. But just like you can't fall off a lake, you cannot fall off a big flat field. A novice can be successful. But driving a semi is more like flying a 747. Is a 747 safe? Yes. But to fly one you'd damn well better know what you are doing.

When Donny and I jump into the waiting truck he doesn't even ask if I want to drive. He takes the wheel. Likely he's not all that excited about riding shotgun with the freak next to him, who's grasping her seat as if on a carnival ride.

On our way home we meet another semi with two people in the cab. "Hey, Don Boy, someone else on their first day of truck-driving apprenticeship," I say.

"Yup," Donny laughs, and we both know my lesson today will start and stay with me as a passenger. I'm better off focusing my efforts on planning farm tours, leaving semi driving in the hands (even if partially wrapped-around-the-wheel and multitasking hands) of my grown-up little brother for now.

Sheets and Lights

Melissa and I took a road trip when we were in our early twenties, before she moved to California. We decided to drive north in her red Beretta. That weekend we would stop at her parents' in Northwood and continue on to Winnipeg to see a Jane Siberry concert. We would sit in Winnipeg coffee shops, surrounded by exposed brick, and scribble in our journals. We would explore obscure streets and marvel at how this foreign city was the same distance from our North Dakota homes as Minneapolis, yet we'd never been here before. We would drive back to Minneapolis, the long way, east through small Canadian towns that reminded us of our hometowns, then south through the Lake of the Woods area, where we would marvel at the folding and unfolding of lakes, more water than we had ever seen, so much blue we could have been island hopping down the Florida Keys.

Before we got to her parents' house, on the first night of our journey, we were on a deserted part of I-29 and almost out of gas. The occasional light of a passing semi came upon us, but otherwise we were in blackness only possible in remote parts of the world. Melissa was freaking out in her hushed way. "Oh dear," she said over and over. Without cell phones back then, if we came to a stop, we were at the mercy of anyone who might decide to help us. While Melissa panicked, I got the giggles after we left the only gas station we could find, which did not yet take credit cards at the pump.

"So. What do we do exactly if we run out of gas?" I asked, trying to remain calm, trying to contain my nervous laughter.

Melissa had me take over the wheel at the gas station, too upset to continue driving.

"I have no idea," she said, knowing her parents were miles away still, and surely deep asleep. Neither of us was keen on the prospect of a semi pulling over to help us, likely our only rescue option.

With every lurch of the car we thought we were in for it. Relief settled upon us as we turned off the highway onto local roads that led to her hometown. We were close, she said. The dark prairie was almost purple now, dotted with the occasional farmstead light.

No matter how familiar the prairie blackness is, I have always been unsettled by it, almost like I could fall into its black abyss if not careful. Then, as if the darkness couldn't handle itself, as if the black was too saturated with blackness, the sky opened. Piercing blue-green rays, the hue of glaciers, reached down from the universe and sliced through the darkness.

"The northern lights!" I gasped. "The northern lights, the northern lights."

Despite our anxiousness to get home before our tank emptied, we pulled to the side of the road and turned off the ignition. While I had caught flashes of the northern lights from a distance before, I had never watched a show like the one before us.

Pillars of light—similar to how it might look to combine giant icicles with splinters of a sunset—illuminated the sky with iridescence. The rays seemed eerily orchestrated, flickering with the same intelligent cadence found in a poem or piece of music. I couldn't judge the light's distance, it was both near and far, in the same way a rainbow seems touchable but you can never reach its base. I imagined Canada putting on this ethereal fireworks show across the border and us—two lone souls in North Dakota—stumbling upon it like blessed witnesses.

As the light bathed us, love overwhelmed me. I felt *her* there, a new woman on my mind, though she was many miles away, in a small yellow house, feeding a child, managing an unhappy husband. I realized there and then that love is like this natural rapture before me: orchestrated by mystery, natural and unexpected, close and untouchable, often born from, magnified by, darkness.

"I think I'm in trouble," I confided to Melissa before our road trip. She and I had worked together for a brief stint after college, before she moved to San Francisco, and we were monitoring the unfolding of my relationship with our mutual boss, Nancy, a woman I fell for instantly, so much so that I thought, *You better watch yourself* the first time she visited my desk after I was hired. What I needed to watch, I wasn't exactly sure. While I felt compelled by this woman, then in her thirties, with brown eyes, straight brown hair, and a strong gaze, any thought of us together was ludicrous. Nancy was married, my boss, and fourteen years older.

"Trouble? Why? Tell me immediately." Melissa and I were walking in a Minneapolis skyway.

"I think something is going on with Nancy."

"Well, what?"

"I don't know, really." At the time this was true. I wasn't sure.

Nancy and I had started talking one afternoon, in the grayness of her cube, thirty-nine floors above the streets of downtown Minneapolis. The afternoon light crawled across calendars and papers as the day transitioned into evening. As the light changed, the Minneapolis skyline began to flicker. I studied her space, the artifacts she chose to display: a picture of her little girl, a watercolor of white lilies in pale-green, sea-glass-tinted Coke bottles, a small tabletop calendar with Georgia O'Keeffe paintings. I knew, somehow, that she was guarded, deeply private. After we settled our business, I straightened my papers, smiled politely, and then asked, "Who painted the flowers? They're beautiful."

She looked over at the painting, lingered for moment, as if reminiscing, contemplating, longing, then she turned, hesitated, and said, "Me."

My image of her, a corporate powerhouse, a manager of a large team, a woman always running to a meeting, changed. "You paint? You're an artist?"

"Yes."

We shifted right then, forever. We began excavating our real selves in the midst of this software company, a spiritual wasteland with depressing corporate politics, meaningless work, lifeless cubes.

Over the next several weeks we exchanged books, shared music, and talked. We talked like starving people feasting after a famine, or like eager flowers rising from the ground to meet the spring sun, or like the ocean tide pulled to the moon. Our words were an unstoppable force. And when we started to dig deeper, opening up about our respective relationships and our spiritual journeys, we'd stop talking and start writing, jotting thoughts on paper and pushing the words back and forth, our truths so raw we were unable to speak.

Many times after work we went to a restaurant in the Warehouse District and sipped wine in the cozy flicker of candlelight. We scribbled questions to each other there too, on the paper tablecloth. At the end of the night we'd fold the paper, shove it into our bags—words expressed but not spoken—and slip from the archaeological dig back to our other lives.

"You are like a lone pine tree, planted at the edge of a desert cliff," I told her, after getting to know her for a few months, "bursting with green, with life, with art and creativity, but rooted in a desert, on the edge of possibility." This was my way to describe the woman I had grown to know who was saturated with beauty, but trapped in a job and life that didn't seem to suit her soul.

Many times I'd arrive at work to find surprises on my desk: a pine cone, blades of grass, leaves, twigs, notes, small sketches, all reminders of the life that beckoned to me too beyond the drabness of the corporate world. We became each other's mirror for what was real, what was neglected in our lives.

I was dating at the time, in my first serious relationship after college, after the wolves. But the woman I was dating did not come to mind as I watched the northern lights. Instead I felt the rising up of the archetypal love Nancy and I shared but didn't yet speak of, a love that didn't need to be chased, cultivated, or manufactured, just channeled. I now wonder if this sort of love lies dormant in most of us until ignited by the right combination of circumstances. Until this organic love finds us, we seek the best substitutes we can find.

Shortly after I met Nancy I dreamed of the tree where at age four I received my message. In the dream I am at the base of the tree, my younger and older selves together in the way dreams blend realities. Nancy is at the tree too, maybe even part of the tree, because she is not represented in body but as energy. I know her energy. And I feel the palpable wisdom of the tree, of nature. I feel all of life flood into me. I feel love.

The dream so moved me that I started to deconstruct my life experiences. Could the early revelation that I would love a woman have been, more specifically, that I would love this exact person? Maybe I felt her, knew her, anticipated her on that day when I was just four years old. Might something have been set in motion before I embodied this life—a divine plan of sorts—and might I have been gravitating toward people with slight fragments of her familiar essence until I met her?

Maybe my journey had nothing to do with being gay, but was about finding love, or even just about finding myself? So when this love found me finally, I realized I had been ignorant in some way. After a short lifetime of secrets, of looking for knowing eyes, of staying in bad relationships, of stumbling through dark bars, I learned that love is simply energy, not necessarily an entity. I learned the lesson I thought everyone in the world needed to learn but me: gender doesn't matter.

But within destiny there is not only poetry and light. There is also darkness, in this case me trying to move out of a relationship, her trying to sort through a marriage, a child, change.

When our lives finally settled, when we could have come together, both single, both open, I left, jumped into another relationship, confused, unsure, not ready.

In the early months of getting to know Nancy, all I knew was rapture. The first time we embraced, everything blended: spirit, body, breath, art, words, friendship, love. Later—was it the first time we came together, or, years later, the second?—we would lie in bed, windows open, on rainy nights and days, smelling the earth, its blossoms and its sweet decay, our bodies close in the way only possible when bodies melt and touch is only about furthering the conversation.

Nancy and I were apart for three years before we got back together. While we were separated I continued to love her completely. I felt at peace—though I couldn't have articulated it at the time—that whether we were near or far apart, our relationship was right because it was authentic. This confidence was striking, in contrast to the way I felt in other relationships where I neurotically tried to make everything work beyond reason. I let my deepest love float away without a fight, while I kicked and screamed to stay in misery.

One random spring evening I invited Nancy to share a bottle of wine I had brought back from Italy. We had done the same before, gotten together several times over the years we were apart, but our dinners were awkward and sad. Both of us silently recalled our connection as we conversed like mere acquaintances.

I had selected the bottle from a tiny wine shop in Tuscany and carefully carried it home. With the wine I brought back the essence of the land: the ancient limestone ruins, fresh bread, savory cheeses, vegetable stands, mysterious monasteries, tropical flowers and fruits on the island of Capri, waves crashing onto the Amalfi Coast, memories of cypress trees, of stone houses, the contemplation of life and death at Pompeii. One cannot help but be in love with life when in Italy. And I couldn't experience Italy, a land saturated with loveliness, without feeling a lingering longing for Nancy. And so, after I returned and settled, I stirred. I stirred throughout the winter, thinking of Nancy. That spring I finally composed a friendly e-mail, inviting her over to enjoy my wine from Italy. She accepted.

And unlike other evenings, as if the wine itself was holy, like the blood of Christ, calling us into a deep communion, we were present and vulnerable. We sat at my round wooden table and talked. Candlelight streaked the darkness of the evening. We shared our lives with the same fresh eagerness we had at her desk so many years before. With that openness, our souls, our bodies, our lives became congruent again, flowing in the same direction.

At brunch, several weeks after we came back together, I looked at her, sitting across the table, moving eggs around her plate, and wondered how this could possibly be: this happiness, this lack of wanting anything beyond the moment, this conversation, this trust, this familiar companionship. And with dread I thought that something bad needed to happen. Something terrible and painful. Nothing can be like this forever, I thought.

Now, here, present: us together for seven years, in each other's lives for fourteen. I pick up a bookmark she gave me early on, within the first several months, inspired by a walk we took. There is a delicate sketch on the front: twisted curls of vine, orange-red berries of bittersweet. On the back Nancy has written:

> going west a place was found
> a patch of nature
> a feeling of serenity
> water, tree, roots, and branches
> life
> eyes deep, thoughts secret

touching a branch, never to be touched the same
taking with us a piece of time
a moment
a place
a love
bittersweet

I often watch Nancy lift a sheet from the laundry basket. She whips it with a precision that always startles me. Then: the snap of the sheet, a fold in half, another snap, another fold, until, like perfect origami, she is holding a neat little square.

I squirm inside when folding sheets. My breath becomes short. My arms don't feel long enough. I can't make the corners match. I can't make my folds geometric. I try for her precision, but end up with a pillow-like rectangle. If she and I were to fold the contents of two baskets together, her final piles would resemble neat shortbread stacked in its plastic package. Mine would resemble smashed marshmallows.

Nancy has folded hundreds of sheets in my presence. With every one she goes into a trance of sorts, focused, dedicated to the exactitude of the fold. And I am always moved. I could just as well be standing by the ocean in ecstasy, waves rushing over my ankles. When I've told her this, she looks at me with a questioning eye. "Odd," she'll say, then return to her project: focus, snap, fold.

While I can't adequately articulate why I am moved by this, it is likely the wonder in watching another human's dedication to perfecting a rudimentary task. When Nancy is folding, I don't exist, the *world* doesn't exist—it is just Nancy, the sheet, and the need for a perfect square. I love her for this selfishness, this obsession.

Watching her in this way, I am reminded of our separate lives, our different paths. Today a contract does not bind us, a house does not bind us, money does not bind us, kids do not bind us, family expectations do not bind us. She lives in her house with her daughter. I live in mine with my cats. Our lives are divided despite my pleading at times for more.

What I was looking for at our brunch, what I anticipated and feared, was the rudimentary, the mundane, the muck of life. And, predictably, we have not been extraordinary. We have been broken, like so many others. But we have embraced the bittersweet. And when our relationship is challenged, the distant memory of the northern lights brings me back to the night I learned that the miraculous is often born from, magnified by, darkness.

Tiny Cowboy Town

I didn't plan this for my harvest retreat, but here I am, belly to the bar and—just like in my work-escape daydreams—sipping my first-ever Schmidt beer. On the stool to my left a stout, older, large-faced man with jowls and dark, leathery skin—and who is missing a finger, I notice—periodically sighs and flaps his lips with uncanny similarity to a snorting horse. Mom, who is on the stool to my right, pokes me when he does this. The bartender, by contrast, is slight, skinny, maybe in his late forties, with raw, boyish eyes and a five o'clock shadow the same color of the auburn grasses outside.

The moonlight dripping over the Sandune Saloon, located in an unincorporated community called McLeod, is the blue-white hue of fairy tales. Sitting at the bar I think of people sneaking through moonlit fields during Prohibition, looking for the amber glow of a small shack in the woods, where they'd push open the door and—for a second—let a gust of warm air, music, and merry voices seep into the night. Like moths to light they'd come.

Melissa would be thrilled at the Sandune. She'd be fiddling on the jukebox behind me, lining up country ballads to fit the ambience of this dark, dusty, cowboy bar. The Sandune would be the perfect performance venue for our opening act, with an audience of three.

And let there be no mistake: this is a *cowboy* bar, according to Mom.

An hour or so ago she and I drove into McLeod on our way home from a café and gift shop in Lisbon, population 2,292. On our way home Mom, at the wheel, asked me if we should swing by McLeod for a minute, to see what there is to see, since it is just a few miles out of our way. Glassy-eyed and tired, staring out of the windows with my feet up on the dash, I responded somewhat apathetically. "Sure. I guess."

Mom is eager to help me find whatever it is I'm chasing here, which I'm not sure is entirely clear to her, since she keeps telling me I'd eventually lose my mind if I moved back.

We turned right at a sign that read "McLeod—3 Miles." A billboard indicated that we were entering the Sheyenne National Grasslands, which is composed of about 70,000 acres and is the only remaining publicly owned tall-grass prairie in the United States. Instead of driving among the familiar patchwork-quilt-like fields of corn and soybeans, Mom and I were weaving through a land of uncultivated, undulating grass. I took my feet off the dashboard and peered out at this new scenery of land flowing freely, wildly.

This was when, noticing my attention, Mom said, "McLeod is a cowboy town."

As rural as North Dakota is, the whole western cowboy thing has never seemed to be a theme in my hometown—and McLeod isn't far from home.

"I don't get it. Why do you say that?"

"Because around McLeod, everyone is a cowboy," she repeated, as if this response clarified.

Winding through McLeod took all of one minute. We passed the Sandune Saloon, the VFW, and an old Standard station that looks to now be serving as both a post office and a general store. A few more buildings stood at the opposite end of town, about two blocks from the bar.

Mom and I pulled up to a white, stately, rectangular box of a building with a pointed bell tower. She shut off the ignition and we stepped out into a world transitioning to twilight. Two dogs barked from a yard in the distance, otherwise the place was quiet—and empty.

After peering into dozens of abandoned buildings over the previous several days, I was not prepared for what I saw through the windows of what turned out to be a one-room school. Wooden desks were lined in two neat rows, six desks to a row. A stack of papers, as if waiting to be graded, sat on a teacher's desk at the front of the room. On the same desk, bookends held several books upright. A chalkboard wrapped around three walls of the room, with a tagboard alphabet above it like a wallpaper border. On one wall a retractable map of the world was pulled taut. Another wall held a majestically framed figure, maybe a president. Two short bookshelves in the back were stocked with books. And a quintessential spinning globe was on a table in the back.

"This place is amazing," I said, and looked over to Mom who was peering in another window. "Think we can go in?" I asked.

I was so mesmerized by how staged the school seemed—like a movie set—that it wouldn't have been beyond me to pop in through a window, with Mom as my accomplice.

"I don't know. Is it locked?" Mom asked, nodding toward the doorknob.

"Uh-huh," I said, pulling at the door.

I was still peering in the windows, looking for a way in, when Mom said, "Is that guy waving?" Behind us, near the barking dogs, a man was standing by an open shed in the back corner of a yard.

"I don't know. What is he saying?" I asked.

"I can't hear him. Maybe he's yelling at those dogs. But I think he waved at us," Mom said.

"Great. He probably thinks we're trying to break in," I said, relieved that Mom wasn't shoving my legs through an open window just then.

"He's probably talking to his dogs. But we can drive that way and see," she said.

We got back in the car and headed in the man's direction. There was nothing inconspicuous about this: Mom's SUV creeping down an empty side road toward the only human in sight. When we got closer, he waved his arms and Mom stopped the car. I rolled down my window.

"You trying to get into the school?" he asked, walking toward us. His tone told me that he was not being accusatory, didn't think we were thieves.

"Yes we are," I admitted. "Do they ever open it?" I'm not sure who I meant by "they."

The man dug in his pocket. He had a rugged look, like that of a lumberjack, with short white whiskers, jeans, and boots.

"Here's the key. If you want to go on ahead and let yourself in, I'll go open a few other buildings you might want to look at too. Then I'll meet you back at the school."

"Other buildings?" I asked.

"Over there in that church is our museum. And the building next to it is a pioneer house." I looked at the small nondescript house he was pointing to. "And you might also look around in the depot station too."

He handed over the key.

"And who are you?" I asked.

"I'm Jay."

"Are you the official building opener or something?" I said, trying to make sense of why this man was giving us, two strangers, a key to the school.

"Well, I guess I am," he smiles. "If I see 'em and catch 'em I am, anyway," apparently referring to curious visitors like Mom and me.

"How many people live here?" I asked.

"There's twenty-six of us," he said with a grin.

We visited for a while longer, and Jay asked, "Where you folks from?"

Mom and I explained that we used to live on a farm between Wyndmere and Barney but had both moved from there. "Thanks for the key," I said. "Guess we'll meet you at the school then?"

"Okay," he said. "I'll see you up there in a bit."

—ww—

For the next hour Mom and I wandered through the McLeod Historical and Preservation Society complex, which was made up of the pristinely preserved school, a Soo Line depot housing train schedules and dozens of old railroad artifacts in glass cases, the pioneer house (as small as a laundry room and furbished as if lived in), and a Presbyterian church stuffed with historical McLeod artifacts, from old magazines to wedding dresses, quilts, farm equipment, and military uniforms.

"Where are we?" I asked Mom. I was shocked at how the entire town seemed to have been freeze-dried, like instant coffee. My hometown has nothing on this order—no museum, no preservation. Old buildings, as far as I can tell, are mostly demolished when they are no longer of use in Wyndmere. McLeod, though, it seemed to me, standing among the stories and artifacts from the past, had people reaching from the blurred edges of time, waving, calling, demanding a stage, demanding to not be forgotten.

In the museum I paged through articles about a teacher who taught in McLeod's one-room school until it closed in 2002. In the eighties she had a spread in *People* magazine and was featured in *National Geographic* due to her status as the lowest-paid teacher in the United States. The story in *People* told of how she had lost her husband in a plane crash and then, three years later, her son in a farmhouse fire. She is also, it turns out, the owner of the Sandune Saloon.

"Mom—why don't we know about this?" I asked, feeling like the last to know family news.

"Oh, maybe I heard something about all that at one time," she responded with a shrug.

"Cowboy hat, Mel," Mom whispers to me when the bartender turns his back to us.

"Yes, I know," I whisper back.

I got a feeling when we entered the Sandune after our self-guided tour of town that Mom might be on to something with the cowboy thing. The inside is dark, with low ceilings, dusty hardwood floors, a pool table, and a black potbelly stove. The bar countertop is covered with hundreds of glued-down pennies. Outside I noticed a stack of firewood on the porch, a touch that—against the backdrop of the rolling grasslands—made it seem like we were in Wyoming.

When he turns back to us, the bartender holds his own beer up and points to the man next to me. "This guy here'd never tell ya, but he raised six thousand dollars for St. Jude's Hospital this year. Held a rodeo with those mini horses of his. Oh—and he stole the Fourth of July parade too. One a dem little horses was pulling him in a buggy," he says. Both the bartender and Jay have mentioned the McLeod Fourth of July parade, which started with Jay and a few others pulling floats down Main Street, just for fun. Now, over four hundred people descend upon this little village every year on Independence Day.

The man next to me shakes his head in a scold, embarrassed at the attention but proud all the same.

"You have mini horses? How tall are they?" I ask.

"Oh, 'bout dis high," he explains. Both of these men have a faint accent common around here, almost Norwegian. He holds his hand above the bar at a height not much taller than an oversized doll.

"How many do you have?" I ask.

"I've got 'bout twenty miniatures." Then, as if trying to give a litter of pesky kittens away, he snickers, "Why, you want some?"

"Yes, I want one in my house," I say, figuring a mini horse might as well be a house pet. And—well, I'm just not that great with bar talk.

"I got one you could get in da house," he says. "She about twenty-ni-i-i-ne, thirty," he says, adjusting his hand above the bar. "Twenty-nine inches. Yup. That one'd fit in your house."

"These are the Hoffert gals," the bartender says, introducing us. "They are trying to eke out a meager living in that wort'less farmland over dere north of Barney."

Mom knows our bartender. I've finally realized that after the bartender says to Mom, "You told me the funniest animal story I've heard in my entire life."

"Are you sure it was me?" she asks.

"Damn, you were funny," the bartender says again. Mom sits innocently. She shrugs her shoulders when I give her the what-is-he-talking-about look.

"Tell me, what is this animal story?" I ask.

"Oh man—you thought the cat was," he can barely speak, "a coat." He puts the back of his hand to his mouth, trying to contain himself. As soon as he says this, the memory of one of my childhood traumas comes back.

At the time I was a stubborn, fierce, independent six-year-old who preferred not to cry and was always right. The event precipitating my trauma was fast and miserable, as death sometimes is. Mom screamed at me to go into the house when it happened, but it was too late. I was already standing in the doorway of the garage, eager to grab a brown Red Owl bag from her arms so I could rush into the kitchen and dig for my cereal.

My body shook as my little kitty flopped around the garage. I had seen only sunfish move in this terrible way after we'd caught them at the lake and piled them on the dock. A sound, a panicked, horrific sound—with the same sudden wrongness of a vacuum sucking up a quarter—filled the air.

Seconds before, Mom had grabbed the last of the packages and slammed the car door. The door hadn't shut properly, though, so Mom had tried again, closing it harder, thinking it was her coat in the way, before she realized she was smashing the kitty's neck. The cat—all black except for a white spot on her head—flipped into a drainage hole in the cement floor and stopped moving.

My remaining memories of the aftermath are blurred: stroking the dead kitty in a shoe box, visiting the grave, crying in my bed, wondering about God and impermanence. The memories faded as time passed and new pets entered my life. At age six I was unscathed, still a new soul until this, my first experience with anguish, with pain and true loss, which, as for many children, came with the death of a companion animal.

The bartender recounts his version of this story, which somehow has Mom heading to church. He goes on to tell the story of our dog Butch. In that story we actually *were* going to church. We were all dressed for church when Butch jumped in the car—leaping from lap to lap—with an eyeball dangling out of his head. Butch had been hit by a vehicle moments before, and, panicked, frenzied, he was looking for comfort, for help.

Growing up on a farm—where pets are often less protected—exposes you to the sometimes messy and imperfect order of the universe.

"You from around here?" I ask Mini Horse, changing the subject. "Yup. Six miles nort' of here," he says.

"Lived here your whole life?" I ask.

"Yup. Got my hair cut in that barbershop across the street when I was a kid."

"Ya, right next to dat grocery store," the bartender jokes, because there isn't a barbershop. There isn't a grocery store. There is, I guess, only a museum complex. The bartender continues. "This place used to have two grocery stores, two implement dealers, three bars, two stockyards."

"And two barbershops. I had my choice!" Mini Horse man jumps in. "One across da street and one across from Millers."

"Well, I think this town has done pretty good compared to Wyndmere, which had a lot more to start with," Mom says.

"Wyndmere. Talk about a ghost town," the bartender says, shaking his head.

"Where's that?" Mini Horse asks.

Mom repeats, "Wyndmere."

"Oh, pluufff," Mini Horse says, shaking his head in disgust, his chops flying.

"Wait, what's the matter with Wyndmere?" I ask.

"Bluhhbb," he snorts, shaking his head again.

The bartender takes a swig of his beer, then says, "When I was growing up, Wyndmere's main street was packed." He starts to rattle off places that have been gone for years—movie theater, bowling alley, and so on—counting them on his fingers.

"Dentist! I had a tooth pulled there," Mini Horse interjects.

Mom adds to the list. "Two hardware stores. A café. And all of those businesses were in Wyndmere when I moved there in 1974. Seventy-four to now, look at how much it has changed."

"Wyndmere is just too close to Wahpeton and Fargo," the bartender says, meaning that there is no way businesses can compete with the larger towns nearby. "Today the highways are nice and the cars are fancy. So: poof. Ghost town," he continues, waving his hand as with an abracadabra.

We all sit for a moment or two, reflecting on change, on the passing of time, when Mini Horse says, rather randomly, "I got a daughter sixty-one and a daughter fifty-nine."

"You are so full of shit," the bartender says.

"No, I'm not full of shit! Born in 1949," Mini Horse says.

"I damn near carded you when you walked in here," the bartender says.

"Oh no, you didn't! You woulda gotten the fist," Mini Horse says.

The bartender thinks for a minute, slams his beer on the table, and roars: "You were not born in forty-nine!"

"I didn't say I was. My *daughter* was!" Mini Horse roars back. "*Geez*, I didn't have kids before I was born. I know that much." Mini Horse takes a sip of his beer, satisfied that he's made a darn good point.

"Well, how old are you?" I ask.

"You guess," Mini Horse says, looking up as if giving us his profile to assess.

The bartender says, "Let's see, when was Custer's battle over?"

"Pflew," Mini Horse says, shaking his head and his chops. "I made up my mind I wasn't going to get married until I was twenty-one. So figure that out."

"Eighty-two," I say.

Mom says, "Eighty-four."

"Did you *have* to get married?" the bartender asks.

"No. I wish I would have!" Mini Horse responds.

I lay out the facts: "Your daughter is sixty-one. You were married when you were twenty-one."

"I'm not sure if she's sixty-one, but I know she was born in forty-nine," Mini Horse says.

"Too much math!" I say, and guess again. "Eighty-one?"

"*You* don't even know how old you are," the bartender growls at Mini Horse. We all laugh.

Mini Horse responds, "That's what people think. People don't think I know nothin', but I don't dare tell 'em what I *do* know."

"Eighty-three?" Mom says.

"That's about right," Mini Horse says. "Enough time that I've been to hell. Know what that's like." I am about to probe a bit, curious what this hell might be, when he says, "I used to ride three miles on horse through the snow to a one-room school house, in fact."

The bartender jumps in: "School had a barn then, didn't it?"

"Yes. And I had girlfriends then. I quit school because I had too many girlfriends. I didn't get any further than seventh grade," Mini Horse says.

"You're a Las Vegas playboy!" the bartender teases.

"How come you remember those good old days? I'd like to forget these bad days." Mini Horse grumbles and spins a bottle in his hands.

"Oh, there's a lot of days I'd like to forget, but a lot of days I cherish too. I went to the Sheyenne one-room schoolhouse. Not the one here in town," the bartender says, pointing somewhere into the heart of the grasslands.

"I remember one time I had to go pee bad," the bartender says. He puts down his beer, backs up, and gives himself room to tell the story. "So I went pee. In a hurry probably." He shakes his head in disbelief. "I was zipping up my blue jeans and, darn it, I caught the end of my peter."

Mom and I start to giggle. "Bad!" he says. "What do you do when you are four years old?" the bartender asks and gives us a big shrug. "You shout, 'Teacher! Teacher!'" He mimics his four-year-old voice and waves his hand in the air. "So the teacher comes. Checks it all out, and says, 'Wait, I'll come back.' When she came back she had a little jar of Vaseline and she said, 'Okay, this might hurt a bit. I'm *gonna* lube up your zipper so it slides easier. On three, you start hanging on.'"

The bartender is looking at us, still disbelieving of his fate. Mom and I are laughing. Mini Horse is making empathetic groans. The bartender starts the countdown: "One. Two. She pulled it on *two*! She lied to me! I was waiting for 'three' and she yanked it on *two*," he says and takes a swig of his beer. "Well, she was in her seventies, so she didn't really turn me on or anything."

"Good thing, being you were only four years old," Mom manages to croak through her laughter.

He continues, "She took a swab of the Vaseline, put a dab on the end of my peter, and sent me back to class."

Mini Horse shakes his head. "Zipper. Got caught in a zipper once. Never forget it."

By this point I have ceased to make meaning out of our unfolding conversation. There is no rhyme or reason and yet it is oddly delightful.

Later, after my harvest retreat, when I am back in my regular life in the city, I'll be around people with egos so palpable that bear cubs could bat them like butterflies in a meadow. When this happens my mind sometime drifts to Mini Horse, whose image appears to me like that of a shaman, flapping his chops. Then come the face and voice of the bartender, howling at the animal stories and talking about his four-year-old "peter" trauma. Jay comes to mind too, handing over the key to his village. And I'll smile to myself, thinking of the rawness of our human imperfection, which, when not masked by egotism and elitism, can be charming, funny, and beautiful. Besides my meeting those characters that night, McLeod is probably such a sweet memory because the entire town is like the last embers of a fire, about to turn from berry red to black. And it is often the last moments of a fire when its warmth is savored the most.

Flow

I'm sitting in the shop on my adopted stool. Coffee is brewing. Its scent is rich, like that of fresh lumber. The world is the purple shade of twilight. I so rarely experience these predawn hours in such stillness that the farm feels eerie and sacred, a land where the cousins of the *huldufólk* might exist.

My ability to sit and observe the simple patterns of a day unfold is luxurious: no conference calls, no e-mails, just the cadence of the farm. My body seems to be finally healing, the pain leaving. And right now I want to stay, not move, and watch the light come and go. But no, I can't.

Before I left the city I made plans for tonight, to drink wine in a farmhouse on the other side of Wyndmere, with a babysitter from my childhood. I sigh and get up to pour my coffee. What had I been thinking?

Jenny, who graduated the year I was in sixth grade, was my idol. She was confident, poised, a cheerleader and a singer, with a melodic laugh and a busy social life. She had a proper disposition that foreshadowed her path to become a teacher, but she also held a persistent smirk in the corner of her lips, as if constantly mystified by the grandness of life. I loved her mostly because she treated me with the respect my twelve-year-old self felt I deserved. Jenny would walk into our house, throw her TV dinner into the freezer, tidy up, and, after she put my siblings to bed, start the stories. She'd tell me about her latest boyfriend, loop me in on high school gossip, and let me stay up as late as I wanted. When I was old enough to watch my siblings, Jenny and I continued our conversations on the school bus, which she rode occasionally. I took my role as her confidant seriously and provided her with therapist-like advice. "I don't know. I'd go for Rodney over Mike," I'd say. Her last year in school I kept a log of her activities in a ruled notebook named the "Jenny Files," and proudly handed them over at her graduation party as a surprise gift.

After attending college, Jenny moved back to Wyndmere, married, took a job teaching at the school, and had four children. While I've always held a fondness for her, we haven't shared more than a hurried hello in the last twenty years. Our short exchanges have been fine with me because to pause, to talk, to get back to our therapy sessions, would mean—as social custom requires when you aren't twelve—that I would need to talk too. And what would adult Jenny—a devout, practicing Catholic and an enthusiastic Republican, with a farmer husband and four kids—say if I told her the truth?

I marvel at the brave ones, those who somehow move like liquid within this world. Whatever situation presents itself, they flow, fill the space, pour into the moment—no fear. Whatever their silences, they've long ago made peace with them. And for someone to take issue with these people, it's just that: someone else's issue. I've cultivated a bit of this flow in my adult life, away from the farm. I rarely shy away from the truth if a stranger should ask me on a plane, "Now, what does your husband do?"—which happens too often. "Well, I don't have one of those." I'll smile and calmly bring up Nancy.

Then, with most people I tell, there is another layer of my story to explain. Nancy and I don't live together. Our lives, while intertwined, are not knotted in the ways that put most minds at ease. Learning this, people—even the most open-minded—will ask about commitment, about next steps, about longevity. I understand their confusion. Over the years I've had to dissociate from cultural milestones as gauges of progress, gauges of love.

Instead, on any given day, during any given year, rather than check off the milestones, I've had to go inward to understand if we belong in each other's lives. My answer has always been yes.

If I could, I would take these conversations further. I'd explain how I can sometimes study a tree and take in its grandeur as if I've just landed on this planet, feeling the awe I might if transported to prehistoric times to experience the immensity of dinosaurs. And within this awe is wonder, and within this wonder is love. And sometimes the smallest details of life—someone caught in a laugh, a breeze that sends ripples over a calm lake—can cause this same love to pulse through me. So, I want to explain, observing Nancy's life stirs this same awe, not because we are knotted but because we are free.

And while I have much to say in my regular life, when I hit the gravel roads—even after all of these years—discomfort settles in me like a persistent cramp. To conceive of acting normal, of talking, of flowing, seems as implausible as using psychokinetic power to scoot a teacup.

Among the professional, progressive, activist, intellectual, academic, and self-realized people I encounter, I can't help but feel embarrassed by the silence I carry back home. I've felt this way around Melissa as our lives diverged and I perceived her becoming the brave one, the hippest among the hip, surrounded by people who seemed to chant, "We're here, we're queer, get used to it" with their very breath. I knew she'd made peace with her parents about being gay and had been back to North Dakota often with her girlfriend. I had assumed all was well in her neck of the prairie—until recently.

A few months ago Melissa and I were in the Lower Haight district of San Francisco, eating at a Pakistani restaurant. She had just finished hosting a radio show from the basement of Black Pancake Records. I had just finished the meetings that brought me to town. We met the evening before, too—we'd eaten burritos in the Mission, caught up on life, and laughed until tears flooded our eyes. Our reunions are sweet and rare.

"When you go home, do you run into many people?" I asked.

"Not really." She paused and swallowed. "Well, I mean—I hide," she said.

"What do you mean, you *hide*?" I asked and set my fork down.

"I mean I don't leave the house if I can avoid it. And if I need to go to the grocery store for something, I run in, grab what I need and run out before anyone can spot me." Plain-faced, she looked at me and repeated, "I hide."

"Shut up."

"Yes, totally. I am so uncomfortable at home, I can't take it."

"So you don't run into people? Old teachers, classmates?" I asked, our shared realities coming into view.

"No. Not really," she said.

"I had no idea. You *do* know I want to crawl into a hole when I go home," I confessed.

"Oh, believe me. I know. It is not normal," she said, and we started laughing out of our own discomfort.

"Wait," I said, now seeing a truer picture of Melissa back home, so different than what I thought, but so like the friend I know. "You really *run* into the grocery store?"

"Hoodie. Shades," she said. I smiled and imagined her ducking into the store as if hiding from North Dakota paparazzi. Then, after a pause, she asked, "What is our problem?"

"I don't know," I said. "Especially after all of these years."

We took a few more bites and thought for a minute. Then Melissa offered, "I suppose the way life is *supposed* to be was so ingrained in us while growing up, we may never get over it."

"Yup," I said. "Probably."

I often think of the family pictures that surrounded me in childhood. Both of my grandparents' houses had picture walls, clusters of faces and stories I studied as the hieroglyphics of how I came to be.

In my parents' wedding photos my dad wears a pale purple suit with a light yellow shirt. While he looks like he might be dressed for a Halloween party, the truth is that he was paying homage to the colors of his softball team, Chuck's Off-Sale. Mom's face is young, the face I remember from the early years, when I watched her breasts hang from her body like half-filled water balloons and I traced the dull pink stretch marks—like Chinese characters—on her soft stomach. The practiced mom I know had barely escaped childhood in the photo.

The pictures of my aunts and uncles hung on the walls too. Time had lapsed, making the photos look like costume shoots: young kids getting together, dressing up, making a run of it. Then from playtime to seriousness, a generation back, in black and white, my grandparents and great grandparents stared at me from lives already lived. First they are captured in their wedding photos; later they are aged, sitting, surrounded by canopies of adult children.

The pictures are like the walls of the Grand Canyon where multicolored layers of rock mark the beginning and ending of ancient eras. I often studied my paternal great-grandmother, Elizabeth, whom people say I resemble. I can see our similarities, sort of. Her eyes are large like mine. Our faces are both narrow, shaped like an upside-down teardrop. In their wedding photo she stands next to my great-grandfather, Jacob. No smiles. I often looked deep into Elizabeth's eyes, searching for her spirit, for our connection. Her union—all of these unions—built the foundation for the next generations, for me.

My siblings and cousins will eventually make it to the family walls, their obligatory wedding photos marking the next layer in our family. Like me I'm sure future generations will study these pictures and trace the unions that established their beginnings. And I—perhaps the most curious about our lineage, the most eager about continuing the stories—will be absent.

I will be missing from the way life is supposed to be.

—◊◊◊—

"I'm heading to Jenny's tonight," I tell Mom over the phone, letting her know I'll be crashing at the farm and not coming back into Wahpeton with Dad.

"That sounds fun, honey. What are you going to do?"

"Drink wine. I'm bringing cheese and crackers," I say. I'm actually bringing balsamic glaze, pesto, Parmigiano-Reggiano, and crackers, which I brought from Minneapolis, worried that my choices here would amount to Velveeta and Wheat Thins.

"Is her family going to be there?"

"No idea," I say, not sure what to expect.

"All right. Have fun," she says. "I'll see you tomorrow."

"I will," I say, though I'd rather be near her, my mom, with whom—though it has taken me nearly a lifetime—I've finally found comfort.

I have heard others talk about time as fast and unforgiving. Days do not politely stop and allow us the courage to deal with all that has gone unsaid. Days don't care. I now know this for myself: years can evaporate as quickly as a morning fog can lift.

Mom and I were on our way to Fargo when I finally spoke openly with her, seven years after trying to talk to her on our gravel-road walk. The moment had selected itself, just like the moment when I came out to her at the Village Inn, or even the night when Dad decided to speak about his mother. None of the times or places had been ideal, but the words still came. Neither was this ideal: a sunny drive to Fargo. Nonetheless, I knew I was going to speak. The silence was revolting in my body, becoming physical, pushing its way to air.

I didn't know what I was going to say exactly. My identity had, in many ways, ceased to be my issue. The real issue was my silence, which persevered like a stubborn throat tumor. But something within me had recently shifted. My love for Nancy started to loosen my silence. I wasn't hiding something that didn't belong on the prairie. Instead, I was full of something as natural and as raw as the prairie.

"Mom."

"Yes."

"Umm." I paused. Familiar fields surrounded us, changing like a flipbook where an animated figure comes alive with the snap of a thumb. Corn replaces wheat replaces beets.

"What is it, Melanie?" She knew something was coming.

We turned from the two-lane highway and onto Interstate 29. *What is it I have to say?* I thought. There was so much, too much, to be delivered in this relatively short car ride: years of relationships, pains, and hidden struggles, how I mourned my separation from my family, the joy and elation I felt with Nancy back in my life. My life as presented to my family, to the North Dakotans, was carefully controlled and calculated. I rerouted conversations like a politician. I slipped out of situations like a magician. If my life was a mansion of rooms, I let my family step into only the foyer and wipe their feet.

"Mom. I—"

"Ye-e-e-s?"

"Don't you think it is strange that I don't talk about my life?" I said in one breath.

"Well, why don't you?" The highway buzzed by. Mom's words echoed in my head. *Why don't I talk?* I didn't have a response. "Well, what do you have to tell me? Just say it," Mom said, before I could respond. Her voice was forceful and confident in a way I didn't recognize.

"I can't just say *something.* I don't have anything specific to report. We haven't talked for years. Don't you think it is odd?" I said as tears came. It is surprising how a close family—one who freely hugs, with a mom who still tells her adult children to be careful of strangers and a dad who watches the Weather Channel just so he can call and ask about the rain in "the Cities"— can avoid each other's true intimacies.

"Melanie. You know you can talk to me. What do you have to say? Spit it out!"

Spit it out? Who is this woman?

"Mom, there is just so much. I don't talk about my relationships. I don't talk about my problems. We are all walking around pretending this is normal."

"What do you have to tell me? That you are in a relationship with Nancy?" Nancy's name, used in this context, brought more tears. I felt the dread of exposure I had run from for years. Yet I also felt an opening in my throat.

"Well, yes. That's one *minor* thing."

"Well, of course I know that, Melanie. What else?"

"I don't know. Everything!" I was almost confused at the conversation. Mom was being matter-of-fact, straightforward. Something had changed or was changing as we spoke.

"When I come home I feel like I have to hide everything. I never talk about my real life."

"And whose fault is that?" Another zinger. *Whose fault was it?*

"I don't know whose fault it is."

"Then talk to me."

"I worry about all of you, what others will say. What the entire town will say."

Cars buzzed by us, others on their way to Fargo.

"Melanie. First of all, do you think that nobody knows? Secondly, I am over fifty years old. Do you think I care what other people think about me?"

"Well, don't you?"

"No!"

"You must be pretty evolved." My tears subsided to the post-cry hiccups.

"I know I am," she said.

"Why don't you ask me any questions about my life—ever?"

"Because *you* don't talk about your life. I want you to feel comfortable. I figure if there is something you want to tell, then you'll say it."

I wanted to gather my words, gather my tears, gather my vulnerabilities. Like a silence hoarder whose silence had escaped, I wanted to round up our conversation and take back my stuff. But for once I didn't. I just let it all be. Our silence wasn't about us anymore, or so it seemed as we sped toward Fargo, it was about me.

At five-thirty I drive into Jenny's yard. Her house is framed by a thick grove of ash trees, ninety years old, she'll tell me. I am surprised to find a yard ablaze: Jenny's husband John looks to be busy with a project; kids are running about, giddy to get a glimpse of the visitor; a chunky old basset hound stumbles around as if she's just lapped some vodka. I somewhat expected a quiet, candlelit wine night (as I'd have with friends in Minneapolis) when—I didn't yet know how—I'd either have to work a miracle to avoid my life, or otherwise confess. The activity in the yard eases my anxiety. How deep can conversation go with a family of six and a pooch in full throttle?

Jenny greets me with a giant hug and helps me manage my platter of cheese and crackers while Dolly, the hound, nudges my shins. When we step into the house I immediately feel comfortable in the way you do when a house is tidy but fully lived in, with evidence of homework and 4-H projects and music lessons. The house has nooks and crannies and corners that catch the late-afternoon sun, like a dream catcher. This is John's childhood home, Jenny tells me, and I am hit with nostalgia, remembering my first house, where the dampness of the earth seemed to bleed from the walls.

After a house tour we settle in the kitchen, spread out my food offering, and open the wine. The rest of the family continues with their regular Friday evening routine, despite us plopped in the thoroughfare. Jenny's kids, three girls and a boy, ranging in ages from six to fifteen, pause to meet me and then come back frequently to engage. "Do you know I babysat Melanie when she was a little girl?" Jenny asks. Jenny's kids consider this fact with amazement. I can see them imagining their mom as a babysitter, and me, this woman in their kitchen, a child. John comes through to say hello too. After a few words he loads a cracker with cheese and leaves to shower.

We have much ground to cover and I drill Jenny with questions: What's life like in Wyndmere? What's it like to work with the teachers who taught us? How in the world do you manage four kids? As she talks, lavishing her response with detail, I realize what drew me to her as a child: this woman is in love with life, with her life, with this life. And this is not just empty bliss. There is a quintessential sparkle in her eyes, which I've come to understand as a playful and irreverent nectar that leaks from some people's souls.

I fill Jenny in on my life too. The years between us give me much to cover and we both avoid topics that would necessitate my big confession. When the kids get into pajamas, Jenny and I move to the couch in the living room. After John shuttles the youngest to bed, he pours a glass of wine and joins us. The world outside is dark now, the house dimmed and hushed. John and I don't know each other well but warm up quickly. The three of us get lost in conversation as if feasting on comfort food. We talk about life in a small town, a recent murder in Wyndmere (an unheard-of event in a town this size), and updates on people I haven't thought of in twenty years. While we talk I can't help but feel some sort of longing. Jenny and John are those who didn't leave this place, my home. Their decision to stay doesn't seem to have been passive but an active cultivation of lives they imagined for themselves.

Near the end of the night I decide to talk openly, to not filter. Maybe I had prepared on some level, having roamed this land for a few weeks, practiced even, after opening up to Joel without sustaining harm. Maybe I am just worn out by my fear. Or maybe I am moved by their humanity, which seems to fill the room with their presence, muting the labels I want to slap on them—Catholic, Republican, North Dakotan—even as I shudder at labels often placed on me.

"Tell me more about your writing!" Jenny says, cupping her wine and pulling her legs into herself on the couch. Earlier I explained I've been writing at the farm. Jenny—an English major, a teacher, a librarian—is interested.

"Well, I'm exploring a few different threads. North Dakota. You know, my crazy longing for this place." They both nod because we've been sharing our affinity for growing up here. "And, ah, I've been writing about how hard it is to come home, since I'm in a relationship with a woman."

John stays still on the recliner. Jenny cocks her head. My words hang in the air. I see that glint in Jenny's eye. John, blurred in my peripheral vision, doesn't move, flinch, or squirm.

"Really? Why is it hard? To come home, I mean," Jenny asks.

I take a deep breath. "Because it is so awkward. I have no idea what anyone thinks. I don't talk about my relationship. And, well, nobody asks me either." As I speak I mirror her calm, though I feel like dry ice is flash-freezing my body. I am the opposite of fluid, like those I so admire. I am sick with vulnerability, which I can only attribute to the practice of holding my truth from this place and these people for over thirty years.

"I've always known that you are you—" Jenny pauses and gives me a careful smile. "I mean, I didn't *know*. But I've always known you. Just you." And this, I take to mean, is that she has always known my essence, just as I've known hers.

We keep talking, except now I color my life fully, introducing Nancy, covering the evolution of my family's reaction, sharing how I just told Joel, and explaining how I wish I could more fully reconcile my life with home. Jenny asks questions. She is curious, but holding back, trying to maintain a sense of normalcy. John stays attentive and nods, letting me know in his own way that all is well. And I—well, I guess I flow.

After the day Mom and I talked on the way to Fargo, my family absorbed Nancy's presence. She was added to the Christmas exchange, pulled into photos, consulted on family matters, and, perhaps much to her dislike, counted on as the dependable one who could track me down when I didn't answer my phone. Her presence also spread into most reaches of my extended family, so that people asked after her as any decent person would, understanding her importance. Over time, I talked with some people in my family, but not all. In some ways we were beyond the need—we were just living the reality. Yet I had not talked openly with North Dakotans outside my family until this trip, until speaking with Jenny and Joel. Still, over the years, I have received a few weddings invitations and Christmas cards from people I've never told, addressed to me with Nancy's first name appended in a gesture of acknowledgement. When these cards arrived I tore them from their wrapper, panicked, not wanting to see.

But why?

Maybe these small and kind signs of acceptance must contend with what is ingrained within me and Melissa and all who hold something that makes them different. Or maybe I have had to navigate a world where language is insufficient, not great enough, where our way of talking about relationships seems suited for cave people governed by sexual impulse, not enriched by the complex energy of our closest companionships. Or maybe in the eyes of those I have never spoken openly to—some relatives, childhood friends, parents of friends—I see myself as I assume they see me: imperfect, lost, a sinner, less than whole. Or maybe, really, beyond all of this, there is a child who holds a prairie silence deeply, fiercely, and believes this silence sets her apart in a way that can never be reconciled.

If only I could believe perpetually in the gifts I've been given from the people of this land—my family, Jenny, and all who would stand beside Melissa and me—and become brave enough to offer my own pictures for the family wall.

The Last of the Barns

"The barn's heading north," Dad says on our commute to the farm one morning, referring to the building's forty-five-degree slant toward Fargo, as if the barn has a mind of its own, is deciding to leave.

Once white, the barn is now almost blue in its grayness. White paint remains in only the creases where the elements can't penetrate. Green moss that appears to be as soft and cushiony as a putting green covers portions of the roof. On the peak, a weather vane spins above the prairie.

The slanting building is the centerpiece of the farm, a nucleus holding together the trucks, tractors, combines, plows, grain bins, augers, and the other buildings in a meaningful order. Should you pass our farm via the dusty gravel roads, the barn is the one building that would leave an impression.

I never get tired of exploring the barn. In the absence of cattle, which we haven't had since I was three, the barn is stuffed with items that must have held just enough value at one time to be spared the burn pit. These items include scrap metal, two-by-fours, tires, broken windowpanes, rusty plow blades, an old freezer, a sink, yellowed hoses, mangled bikes, and doors salvaged from houses that no longer exist.

Over the years I have been hardly able to make my way through the junk to the back corner of the barn, where light illuminated a worn punching bag that hung from one of the rafters. I'd give the bag one big wallop and imagine my uncles as teenagers pounding the bag, beads of sweat carving tiny rivers in their dirt-covered bodies.

When Dad and I arrive on the farm today I decide to spend my day focusing on the barn. I find that the punching bag is gone—Dad doesn't even remember it being there—and the windows where light used to filter through are glassless.

Inside and directly to the left is a narrow stairway that steeply ascends to the loft. I climb to the second floor like I have for years. Up here long boards are scattered about, with rusty nails sticking out inconspicuously. Massive amounts of pigeon poop coat this level like frosting, and basketball-sized holes, through which feed used to be dropped to the cows below, are hard to spot in the mess. One could step on a board, slip, and step into a hole easily. And the beams holding this floor, its junk, and me are leaning—like Dad said—dramatically to the north. I'm not certain how safe my exploration is these days. But I am drawn to this place like a kid to a tree house.

Back on the ground floor, under the stairway, I peek in a small room where remnants of childhood bikes lie in a pile. Most of them are from a time before my generation, Schwinns with blue handlebars. When I was growing up, animals chose this room as a birthing center. I would check here for new kittens and puppies as small and naked as baby moles.

"Be careful. I think there are a few dead cats in there," the voice of my brother warns.

I turn to find him in the barn, curious, I'm sure, at what I'm up to today. I've gotten the sense that I might be entertainment on the farm, something for Donny to check up on from time to time—a diversion.

"What do you mean, dead? Did someone murder them?" Rage rises in me. I know the unspoken secrets of farm life, how unwanted cat or dog populations are "managed."

"No-o-o," Donny rolls his eyes. "Who knows what happened. They could have eaten poison. Or froze," he says, as if these scenarios are any better.

I always assumed Grandpa built the barn for the cattle he kept in the early years until I was three. I never thought to question otherwise. But a few years ago Dad told me that the barn had actually been built by a farmer who lived on the farmstead before our family did. By extension, the barn is over a hundred years old. I never thought to ask about the barn's beginning. If you don't ask on the farm, information isn't posted on bulletin boards waiting to be discovered.

When Dad has talked about demolishing the barn, I'd go nuts. "Dad. Please don't. How could you destroy a building with so much meaning and history?" I'd whine. For me the barn embodies a prairie history beyond my family. Its disposal will be irreversible—a physical sign of change.

This history argument holds absolutely no weight with my dad. He's not sentimental in this way, does not linger on the past. Old stuff, in Dad's mind, means less efficiency, more work, more to repair. But for me the barn is what makes the farm so—"farm-y."

Today, though, studying the outside of the barn, I realize that a fierce storm may knock the last breath out of it if Dad doesn't get to it first.

"It's coming down in November," Dad says behind me on his way to the shop.

A rebuttal would be worthless at this point, and I can for the first time appreciate the hazard Dad must address. "Pottery Barn would kill for the wood" is all I say.

"They can come and get it then!" he growls, sick of hearing yet another idea of what we could do with the barn.

I have wondered if there is any way I could single-handedly save the barn. My plans have ranged from transforming it into a giant living space with high ceilings and a gourmet kitchen, to starting a Save My Barn campaign to solicit donations from people who care.

Later that afternoon I glance at my e-mail and see a link in my news feed, "10 Amazing Homes You Won't Find in Your

Neighborhood," by Diane Tuman. I click on the link and then notice, among several unusual living quarters, a white barn that looks like ours. The paragraph under the image reads:

> This Bainbridge Island, WA barn was built 104 years ago and was used as a dairy farm before being converted into a home. It retains its barn shape with soaring, cathedral ceilings with exposed beams and rough-hewn floors. Rolling barn doors serve as shutters to two bedrooms and one original wall reveals the original penciled shopping list that includes 2,100 pounds of seeds. Sixteen windows in the open living area draw passive solar heat and natural light.

The Bainbridge barn recently sold for $542,000, the article says. "Thanks, Diane," I whisper, annoyed. Soaring cathedral ceilings with exposed beams? *Exactly what I was imagining! Yes, please.* Rough-hewn floors. *Yes, please.* But—half a million dollars? Even if I had the funds, my parents would lock me up for spending that kind of money on the barn. This represents another difference between people who can buy land and space (and barns) for recreation and relaxation and those who work the land as a way of life. Here a barn is a barn—at least with my family.

"Dad, what can I use to pull wood from the barn?" I ask, locating Dad in the shop after I read about the Bainbridge barn. Dad pauses, looks up and tilts his head back and forth as if weighing options. He walks to a wall where a bunch of crowbars cling to a long magnetic strip, and he removes three of them, small, medium, and large. Then, from another wall, he grabs two hammers.

"Try these," he says, placing the tools in my arms like he is assembling a layer cake.

Back at the barn I let the tools fall to the ground in a clamor. "All right. Here we go!" I say, rubbing my hands together.

I have no idea what I'm doing.

On the south side of the barn I pick a beautiful board that runs half the length of the building. The wood has swirling knots and is decorated with lichen the color of rust and mint. For a few minutes I stare at the board, feeling a deep resistance to defacing the barn. While it is falling apart on its own, ripping pieces from it will speed up its demise. Yet I want to take parts of the barn with me. I don't trust my family to preserve pieces of it, even at my request.

With a tap of my hammer, the straight edge of the medium-sized crowbar fits in the hairline gap that runs horizontally between the boards. Moving down the length of my chosen board, I pound the bar in at every two feet. When I do this, the wood pulls from the building by about a quarter of an inch, and this pull releases the nails by a few millimeters. When I've gone the length of the wood, I go back and push the boards to the frame so the nails stick out. Next I hook the nails with the curved end of the crowbar. The wood is brittle, so I remove the nails with the same diligence and patience I imagine is required for an archaeological excavation. After about an hour the board comes free.

Next I move to the window frames and apply my method: pound the crowbar between two pieces of wood, wiggle the bar until I gain a bit of space, release the crowbar, push the wood back in place, delicately fish nails out of the wood. I excavate three window frames, which I plan to use to make mirrors.

For the rest of my harvest retreat I return to the barn to partake in my own small-scale harvest of barn wood. After a few days of working on the barn I can see the young, tan, muscular hands of the men who built the structure. In my mental picture they are nailing the boards that I am now—over a hundred years later—removing.

I've had a recurring dream where I'm wandering down the gravel roads by the farm. I take a right down grassy tire tracks that run along a cornfield and travel under a canopy of cottonwood trees.

In real life, this road ends where the trees are so overgrown a vehicle can no longer make its way ahead. I have driven to this spot many times, parked my car, and wandered into a particularly thick grove of trees between the road and the field. The space was someone's farmstead at one time. A withered farmhouse is hidden within the thicket. A shed and a railroad car sit several yards from the house. How or why a railroad car was brought to this place, I have no idea. I have always liked the fact that it was there—that all of the buildings were there—unexpected.

In my dream, when I turn into this same farmyard I am at the entrance of a hidden town. The town has a main street lined with little shops and houses. The edges of the town are somewhat wild, bleeding into the fields and disappearing into the woods. I am always elated in the dream to have found this haven, this place of people and community, surrounded by woods and fields. Somehow in this dream I am in all worlds at once. I am in a blended homeland.

Jessica and I are now dear friends, my passion for her a memory, a story. When in college I finally confessed my feelings, which had fortunately subsided by that time, it took her a bit to adjust, think, and remember again. Since then we've shared stories of great loves (hers of men), broken hearts, and lifelong dreams. True to her ever-present adventurous spirit, after stints in the Peace Corp, then living in Colorado and Montana, she moved to Alaska where she now travels in small planes to inlet villages and works with kids who have speech, language, and literacy difficulties.

On a hiking trip in the Grand Canyon several years ago, Jessica and I were resting with a ranger who lived in the area year-round. We were at a picnic table and he was explaining his passion for the place he called home.

"When I look around at the canyon walls I realize how insignificant a generation, a lifetime, or even a thousand years is," he said. "These rocks were formed over millions and billions of years. Can you even comprehend that? Honestly, I see no reason to pay attention to politics. I barely pay attention to who the president is. We think everything is such a big deal, but in the scheme of things our time here is nothing. All we have is what we surround ourselves with. That's why I live here. You should always live in a place you are crazy about," he said.

His words haunt me today. I knew then, as I do now, that I had not been deliberate about where I would make my adult home. I simply followed the migratory pattern of rural kids, moving to the nearest city in search of something I couldn't find in the middle of nowhere. And now, where I live, I miss all that can't be had *except* in the middle of nowhere.

On the last few days of my harvest retreat I establish a pattern. I get up early, watch the sunrise from the shop, brew my Folgers, listen to Joel's show for harvest updates, and set up a writing space. Once settled I write, capturing my harvest retreat stories. When I need a break I pour coffee into an insulated mug, throw on my jacket, step out, take a deep breath of the familiar, corn-drenched air, and head to the barn where I continue my project of removing boards and window frames. Dad and Donny pop up from time to time, visiting me near the barn or in the shop, keeping tabs on my activity.

A month has given me just enough time to fully settle into a different mind-set. I am a writer here. I am a farmer here. I am living on the land here. I have time for people here. I think of Joel, Jenny, the Sandune Saloon gang, and others I've encountered during this time.

But the harvest retreat is about to end.

On my last evening at the farm I stand in the driveway and study the barn, trying to memorize its physical form and how I feel near it. The moon lingers just above the roof, a large white ball, as if a prop placed by a photographer seeking a perfect shot.

I have noticed dozens of leaning and sinking barns while exploring around home—dozens of barns *leaving.* And they won't be coming back. In place of our barn, an aluminum machine shed will go up. This is the same elsewhere. People don't build wooden barns any more—they build aluminum pole barns. The landscape is changing.

When I come home again, the archetypal view of the farm—a barn and this harvest moon hovering so close it feels like I'm in space—will likely be changed, the barn gone. In fifty years, more barns will be gone, more small towns will be dead, and fewer kids will grow up in space and silence. I am sad but also feel like a witness.

As I memorize the barn, the questions I've carried on my harvest retreat rattle in my heart: Could I return home? Can I reconcile my silence? What am I losing by not being here? What is everyone losing?

Somehow, standing at the barn, I know the timing of its demise is not random. Somehow I know as I say goodbye to it that I'm saying goodbye to more than a building. Somehow I know that the pieces of the barn that tomorrow I will collect, power wash, lay out in the sun to dry, and pack into the back of my car are more symbolic than practical, as much as I try to convince myself that I can build a bookcase. Somehow I know, though I haven't said it out loud, that I am standing in the land of my past, in the land of my childhood, not the land of my present. Somehow I know that I am forever one of the in-betweens: those who leave, but never truly leave, because our families are rooted in the community like the trees are rooted in the earth.

Here—at the edge of North Dakota, at the edge of irreversible change, at the edge of my silence—I realize that I have already lost so much. I've lost years of sharing the truth with my family, years of allowing people like Joel and Jenny to enter my life, years of living in a place where my soul is stirred by sunrises. By the barn I know that finally, truly, utterly it is time to reconcile my silence. I know my family is not the problem. The fact that I am in a relationship with a woman is not the problem. Instead, there is something deeper. Something that keeps people who walk this land close to each other in a way where they are ready to plow a neighbor's driveway, deliver a hot dish to a grieving family, and harvest an ailing farmer's field in a moment's notice, but that makes them unable to give voice to their deepest feelings. There is something that silences the stories of lives, lives like my grandmother's as well as mine, and something that pushes those who cannot stand the silence away from the beauty that was once their childhood home. And maybe this something—whatever it is—is the same as it is everywhere. But perhaps it is harder to avoid where I am from, because to live in this land is to be known. One cannot be anonymous.

Perhaps I needed distance from the landscape of my beginnings to find the strength to finally share my story with the quiet people of the prairie who may have been ready to hear it all along—and who probably have their own stories to share.

Epilogue: Going Home

"Foggy there last week?" Dad asks over the phone.

Foggy? I think for a second. Dad often calls to see what the jet stream has pushed east into Minneapolis. I'm sitting at the dining room table and catch a glimpse of my suitcase sitting by the door.

"Ah, you know—I'm not sure, actually. I was in New York last week. But now that you mention it, I think the pilot said something about fog when we were preparing to land. Why?" I ask and step into the kitchen to rummage for a snack.

"It was foggy here. Made for a good fire," Dad says.

"Why's that?" I ask as I reach for a bag of almonds, not sure what fog has to do with fire.

"The fog was so thick it hid the smoke."

"Oh, yeah? What did you burn?" I ask.

"The barn," Dad says.

I drop the almonds, leave the cupboard open, and sit back at the table. A swift pang of grief nests in my heart. "What do you mean you *burned the barn?*"

"When I saw it was going to be a foggy day, I decided to get Caterpillar out here." I hear pride of ingenuity in his voice, thinking to conceal a fire whose magnitude would have drawn unnecessary attention from neighbors who'd follow the smoke to make sure everything was okay. "We pushed the barn over into a pile," he continued. "Then I sprinkled a little gas and lit a match. Burned good."

"Why didn't you warn me, so I could be there?" I ask in protest, though I know it is of no use. I can almost hear the crackle of the brittle wood—bone-dry for decades—as it pops before rising as smoke to disappear into the fog. I think about the final days of my harvest retreat, how I spent hours at the barn's side, using crowbars to loosen what I could. The pieces of wood I brought from the farm and stacked in my garage seem so small and insignificant now. I had wanted to do more, reclaim more, before the barn was gone. I wanted the pillars. I wanted the beams. I wanted the floorboards. I had thought that when Dad finally decided to take the barn down the process would take days. I had thought I'd be there.

"I couldn't warn you because I decided to do it that day," Dad answers. "Because of the fog," he adds.

"You didn't plan it?"

"Nope."

"The barn is completely gone?" I ask, shocked.

"Yup. All that's left is a small burnt pile."

After I left North Dakota after my harvest retreat the barn had remained intact, despite Dad's threat that it was coming down in November. As the weeks and then the months passed, I had thought that not asking about the barn would somehow protect it, even though from time to time Donny would warn, "You better get out here. I don't think it will be much longer." But when I didn't get the call, I remained hopeful that how I left the barn, leaning and moon-soaked, would be the end of the story.

"Dad, aren't you the least bit sad?" I ask, wondering if this change somehow stirs his younger self. The barn had been the only remaining original farm building. The other sheds, bins, and fences I knew from childhood had met this same fate years ago.

"I've got enough in the present to keep me occupied—"

"Without worrying about the past," I finish his sentence. "But Dad, doesn't the yard seem sort of, you know, empty?" I ask, imagining how it will feel to see a bare spot where the barn used to sit facing the world.

"Nope. It's nice and open now," Dad says. "I like it that way."

After we hang up I shake my head in disbelief. The barn is down, but there is more that is delivered with this news. Though it could have come on any random day, Dad's call has come just as I am about to hand the final draft of this book to the publisher. Over the last several months, as I've written, I have contemplated the ultimate lesson of my harvest retreat. What had I gained if not the revelation that I should pack my bags, leave the city, and move back home? And now, hearing about the barn, I realize my lesson is deeper. My lesson is about letting go, embracing fear, and allowing for change. All these years I've tried to contain my story, to hold my truth close. The barn is down. But, more importantly, this book is done. When the fog lifts, when what I've concealed is no longer hidden, it will be time to embrace the open clearing. It will be time to build something new. Only then can I find my way home.

Acknowledgments

I am abundantly grateful to all who have supported my writing in thought, word, and deed, even though—for now obvious if irrational reasons—I often made it challenging for people to help. And so, with a deep breath and feeling of release, I send thanks into the world to my immediate family: Mom, Dad, David, Chrisy, Donny, April, Jarrod, Julia, and the little ones you have brought into being, and also to my extended family of Thiels and Hofferts (and the branches within both); I can't imagine what my life would be without your love. I thank the Kaysens, a clan of people I adore. I thank Barrie Jean Borich and Patricia Weaver Francisco for your advice, insight, and faith in my writing, and others at Hamline who have helped me along the way. To Amy Brandzel, Ryan Knoke, Montana Scheff, Kristin Antoniotti, Heather Dawley, Shannon Horton, Murray Sagsveen, Kristi Sagsveen, Corinn Sagsveen, Stephanie Zhong, Natalie Kawai, and Krista Wiger: thank you for supporting my work, especially those of you who read parts of the manuscript and offered feedback. Thanks to Melissa Maristuen, my famous DJ friend, for coming into my life at the right time and staying. To Danielle Thompson, for everything, especially for being my lifelong, dear friend. To Wendy Sherman, my agent, for finding the perfect home for my first book. To Gayatri Patnaik, my editor, for your kind guidance, and to everyone at Beacon, for your enthusiasm. Thanks to all at Teach For America, especially my team, for supporting my writing schedule, which made it possible for me to make substantial progress. To the wonderful people of North Dakota, especially those in the book, named and unnamed. To Donny, Dad, Mike, and Jake for letting me be a "farmer" during harvest. I'm sure you've never had so much fun. (Right?) And to Nancy for reading every word as if it were new, even after countless revisions over countless years, but especially for all the ways you bring beauty to this world, beauty that has cracked open my life—a story that altogether deserves its own book.